What others are saying about
The Implementation Code

"When I want clarity in my business, I turn to Stacy. When I'm feeling overwhelmed in my life, I turn to Stacy. She has this seemingly 'magic power' to make complicated things simple and... dare I say... fun. If you want to tap into this magic for your own business and life ... READ THIS BOOK!"
~ Chris Winfield
aka The Super Connector™

"Stacy's mind is a brilliant work of art. She masterfully articulates her systems and processes, and I've been lucky enough to experience her expertise personally. More than anything, she's someone I trust to GET IT DONE. Her conversations are enlightening, and I'm thrilled to see her sharing her knowledge to help entrepreneurs get to the next level."
~ Jasmine Star
Photographer + Business Strategist + Founder of Social Curator

"As a busy entrepreneur, I don't have time to read books that don't get practical about time management. That's why I FREAKING LOVE Stacy's book. She isn't content to just give you some big ideas that you've read a million times. She gives you real, concrete steps to begin implementing in your life right away. Better yet, she focuses on changing your mindset so that there can be lasting change. Many of these steps I've already started using to get more done. You absolutely MUST buy this book."
~ Allie Casazza
Host of "The Purpose Show"

"It's not rocket science AND it works – two things I can get behind when it comes to any strategy! Stacy's no fluff, no-nonsense, straightforward approach to getting things done is exactly what all entrepreneurs need. Stacy gives you the direction and inspiration that you need to get into motion and accomplish everything you desire for your life. A must read!"

~ Amy Porterfield
Entrepreneur and Host of "The Online Marketing Made Easy" Podcast

"Stacy Tuschl has nailed it. The first and only book I've seen specifically for business owners that's focused on our #1 problem! The step-by-step advice within will benefit any entrepreneur, no matter what type of business they run."

~ Ali Brown
Entrepreneur, Mentor + Founder of The Trust

"*The Implementation Code* truly IS the secret to getting it all done! It is a new way of solving a very old problem: time management. A world of success and productivity awaits those who would read this book and be inspired by it to take action!"

~ Julie Solomon
Business Coach and host of "The Influencer" Podcast

"This book is your go-to guide for making real progress in your existing or dream business. We all have big dreams, but the big pile of laundry or even bigger day-to-day grind often gets in the way of making real progress. We all start our dream business with the hope that it will provide freedom, flexibility, and a stress-free income. What most of us end up with is a 24/7 job that completely runs our life. I devoured *The Implementation Code* in one sitting, spent the next two days re-evaluating my business, and finally feel re-centered. Stacy shifted my mindset, gave me the tools and strategies to take immediate action, and pulled me out of overwhelm and in to action mode. If you're ready to make a solid income doing the work that actually lights you up, this is a must-read."

~ Britt Seva
Social Media Strategist and Host of the "Thriving Stylist" Podcast

"If you've ever said to yourself, 'There's not enough hours in the day' or 'I just don't know where to start,' Stacy Tuschl has written the guide for you to get off that strugglebus, sister. She's a powerhouse of knowledge and has unlocked the keys to getting it all done and getting back to loving your business again. If you're tired of the hustle and the never-ending to-do list, *The Implementation Code* can get you to the other side of that hustle, and there is so much more there for you, my friend."

~ *Jennifer Allwood*
Best Selling Author, **Fear Is Not the Boss of You**

"Stacy Tuschl gets more done in a day than most get done in a week – I am continually impressed with what she is able to accomplish. With *The Implementation Code*, she has created a guidebook for anyone to feel more accomplished while scaling their business. Whether you are just starting out or if you are running a multi-million-dollar company, the strategies and tips on how to streamline your days will create a strong foundation for your business to scale with ease."

~ *Tonya Dalton*
Best-selling Author of **The Joy of Missing Out** *and CEO of inkWELL Press*

"Stacy is a recognized business leader in both the online and offline space that excels in accomplishing massive undertakings in minimal time. *The Implementation Code* gives you the insider's playbook on how to accomplish what you want, when you want it done, and without the stress, strain or struggle along the way."

~ *Kelly Roach*
Founder, The Unstoppable Entrepreneur

The Implementation Code

Unlock the Secret to Getting It All Done

By Stacy Tuschl

Business Coach | International Best-Selling Author

The Implementation Code
Unlock the Secret to Getting It All Done

Published by Victory Books Publishing
10001 St. Martins Road
Franklin, WI 53132

ISBN: 978-0-9968104-3-2

Cover design by Jim Saurbaugh | JS Graphic Design

whether personal, financial, or otherwise, that is incurred as a consequence, directly or indirectly, from the use and/or application of any of the contents of this book.

To my family: Thank you to my husband, Kent, and my girls, Tanner and Teagan, for always being so supportive, helping mom get it all done.

To the implementer: You are one new habit, boundary, or system away from having the life you've always dreamed of. I am honored you have chosen me to help you take action and get it all done.

Table of Contents

Introduction

It's simple. All success comes from getting things done. However, when it comes to actually getting anything done, from the smallest task to launching a business or entrepreneurial enterprise, there is no shortage of stumbling blocks, speed bumps, and obstacles that can pop up at the start or along the way that may delay or even derail your efforts. My goal in writing this book is to help you learn how to get past those challenges (or avoid them altogether), so those things do not become brick walls that stop you completely.

Perhaps you know people who seamlessly move forward, knocking out their to-do lists efficiently and effectively. Every. Single. Day. There seems to be no stopping them, and you wonder how they do it and wonder why you can't replicate their efforts. Many of my clients have asked, "Stacy, how do you get so much done all the time?" When I'd repeatedly heard the question, I realized I had to share my secret. Okay, it's not really a secret. It's a process. I use it consistently to take action and move forward... aka "get things done."

There are two different situations to consider as we begin, and if you're like me, you've probably already encountered both of them.

Situation #1

First, I live near this huge furniture store, and if you live anywhere near a major metropolitan area, you probably live near the same one, too. They're known for really reasonably prices and offer a huge selection in styles and colors. Additionally, their furniture is proven to stand up to a lot of wear and tear with solid engineering behind it.

You've walked through the doors and are directed to the showroom, complete with arrows pointing the best direction to follow so you don't miss a thing – living rooms, bedrooms, bathrooms, kitchens, kid-specific furniture, desks and office furniture... you name it, they offer it. And you find the perfect piece. It's available in the right wood tone, the right size, and it will perfectly match your home decor. You check the attached tag and see you're now directed to Aisle 10, Bin 27 in the warehouse.

Once you land in Aisle 10 and discover Bin 27, you quickly realize that you'll be the one doing the assembling... and you'll have to lug the carton home. You think, "How hard can it be? It all goes together with an Allen wrench, right?" Although you're not wild about the idea, you think about the great price and how perfectly it is going to work in your home, so you drag the carton onto a cart and proceed to check out.

You arrive home and unload the carton, already feeling a bit frustrated about the do-it-yourself assembly and overwhelmed when you see the various pieces but can't envision how they're going to fit together. But you're smart, so you immediately refer to the instructions and are even smart enough to take inventory of all the pieces as itemized on the instruction sheet before jumping into the assembly process. And that's when you realize that the bolts and the Allen wrench are missing.

It stops you in your tracks, and you don't attempt the assembly because you know that crucial items are missing.

Situation #2

You have a subscription to one of the meal delivery services – the ones that send you all the ingredients, pre-measured in the exact amounts that allow you to cook a healthy and delicious meal without having to research what's needed, trek to the grocery store to buy it, and then measure accurately. If you're not a great cook or don't particularly enjoy cooking, the service is perfect. It enables you to prepare a meal for your family or friends that is delicious, healthy, and may even have restaurant-quality "presentability." Far better than slapping something together out of your refrigerator or pantry.

It's Sunday night, the end of a busy weekend. You're a bit tired, but you're also looking forward to a nice meal. You've saved the meal for just this occasion. It'll be a great way to end the weekend. You open the box and find that all of the necessary ingredients are in place. (Whew, not like the furniture fiasco!) However... the recipe and instructions are missing.

Okay, you can wing it, trying to figure out what gets sautéed, broiled, or baked – at what temperature and for how long – and using your best guess to determine when ingredients are added in the process. You may end up with something edible even if it doesn't look quite like the picture (or it might go in the trash and you call for pizza), but it likely won't be the meal you were anticipating, and if you were planning to serve guests, you won't come off looking like you knew what you were doing in the first place. Uh-oh.

Making It Work

In situation #1, you were missing tools and pieces, so success is improbable at best (and not without a lot of stress and struggle) but more likely quite impossible.

In situation #2, even with all of the right ingredients and pieces (aka tools), you didn't know the order in which they needed to be added and used or the specifics about preparation. Tools only work if you know how to use them and in the proper order.

With *The Implementation Code*, I am going to provide you with all the tools and the recipe and instructions you need, so you can achieve success… and get things done! While I'm going to give you tools and clear, implementable instructions, let's face it, you are the one who actually has to do it. You are the one who has to take action.

Unfortunately, per Quora.com, statistics show that "only 60 percent of books purchased are ever opened. And that says nothing about whether they are even finished." (https://www.quora.com/What-percentage-of-the-books-bought-in-America-are-really-read)

Additionally, even fiction best sellers have less than a 50-percent completion rate. So congratulations for at least opening this book and starting to read! You're already ahead of the pack. You've taken the first step.

Similarly, online courses (even those offered by Harvard and MIT) have rather dismal completion rates – as low as 15 percent. (https://www.insidehighered.com/digital-learning/article/2019/01/16/study-offers-data-show-moocs-didnt-achieve-their-goals)

Keep in mind that there has already been a financial investment in paying for the course, yet those who've invested don't do what's needed to finish. E-learning has exploded, but that's not necessarily making us any smarter. We have to take action. We have to get it done.

Why Me?

In working with my clients, "getting things done" always seems to be the regular speed bump if not an outright stumbling block. It's the very reason I wrote this book. Entrepreneurs are busy people. I understand that. Entrepreneurs also want to build businesses that support the lifestyles they want. I get that too.

From the moment I graduated high school, I have been working toward creating the life I want, and today, as I sit here and write this, life is really good. I have two really successful businesses, investment properties, am writing my second non-fiction book, just completed a children's book, and was recently named the Wisconsin Small Business Person of the Year. After 15 years, my husband and I have a solid marriage – not only do we love each other, but we still actually like each other – and we have two daughters, ages 7 and 4, so you know we're busy. I'm in the best shape of my life and financially in better shape than I've ever been.

I'm not saying any of these things to boast. I'm sharing this because 18 years ago, none of this existed. I created it by taking action and implementing – things I'm going to share with you, so you can also design and create the life you want for yourself.

Very often, people tell me that I'm very self-disciplined and they perceive me as a perfectionist. That makes me laugh because I would never describe myself as either of those things. I simply know how to get things done.

Additionally, I have always taken time to learn from people who are smarter than I am. Nothing I will share in this book is completely and uniquely out of my own head. I didn't make it all up.

What I have done is read hundreds of books, listened to a bazillion podcasts, bought online courses, invested hundreds of thousands (yes, you read that right) of dollars in coaching. I have taken all of that information and tweaked it and refined it in my life, and that's what I'm about to share with you. Every bit of information can be taught and learned. There is no one reading this book who can't take this information, implement it, and replicate success.

In the case of *The Implementation Code*, you'll have to keep reading to learn, but I promise that you'll find the book easy to read, and we'll start with a 10,000-foot view about your mindset to help you uncover why you currently aren't getting things done and then continue to drill down to the specifics – the nuts and bolts – of ways in which you *can* get things done.

> *"The more I practice, the luckier I get."*
>
> *~ Arnold Palmer*

It's like any new endeavor or habit. Think dieting or making a New Year's resolution. We say we want certain things, but our actions and the resulting outcomes suggest something different. It all starts with taking action, but to really stay on track, you have to understand your own mindset and what may be holding you back in the first place, so let's jump in and get started!

Chapter One:

What's Holding You Back?

I'm pretty sure I know you. You're already a high achiever and are the proverbial "go getter" who wants to do it all. You're an entrepreneur and you have big goals... goals that you really want to achieve. Goals that are worthy of your efforts and expertise. Life-changing things. Entrepreneurs have a ton on their plates. If you happen to also have a family, multiply that ton by about ten. There is no shortage of things that have to be done, from daily tasks to taking massive steps to make your goal a reality.

So when you want to get more done but aren't, when things aren't crossed of your to-do list, there's a question to answer: Why aren't you making the decision to commit and take action? In this chapter, we're going to work to release whatever it is that's holding you back.

I can actually answer the question *Why aren't you making the decision to commit and take action?* The answer is one simple word: you.

Please... don't immediately disagree with my assessment or offer any excuses. "My spouse doesn't support me." Or "My staff is still learning." Or "I'm doing it all myself because I can't find the right people for my team." Or "I'm striving for greater work/life balance." (And on that note, I'll share an important tidbit: When you learn to implement correctly, creating work/life balance solves itself.)

The reason we may fail to commit and take action is on us, and creating self-awareness is what we need to tap into first before we get into any specifics or logistics. Your mindset comes first, and without the right mindset, you'll continue to struggle to get things done.

Your brain is always interpreting the outside world and everything that happens around you. That interpretation can negatively impact how fast and far you are able to go. I want you to hear what's normal, so when you experience the things that hold you back, you'll realize they're a normal part of setting and achieving a bigger goal. Sometimes, when you're in the thick of things, it's difficult to focus on the bigger, better picture. For example, perhaps as a new parent, all you experience are the ongoing sleepless nights, and you're exhausted. You can only focus on the next few hours. You're not sure how you'll get to tomorrow. Then you hear from other parents that things start to improve after about six weeks or so. The baby gets into a routine, so things go more smoothly. It helps improve your expectation and experience (after all, you're a first-time parent and have never done this before), so you realize this is simply part of the process and you know you have to keep going… so you do.

Some part of you picked up this book because you want to get more done than you currently are doing. You might not be doing anything, stuck in the daily routine and unable to break out of that rut. Or you might be crushing it and getting a ton done, but you want even more. No matter who you are or the stage at which you find yourself right now, you want to accomplish more, but for whatever reason, you haven't been able to achieve that. I know that or else you wouldn't be reading this book.

First, acknowledge that, of course, you don't know how to do something you've never done before. That is completely normal. As kids, we accept that there is a lot to learn; however, it seems when we become adults, we think we should already know it all. How in the world could you know how to do something you haven't done yet? I can't tell you how many of my clients feel shame, guilt, or embarrassment when they turn to me for help. I hear, "I should know how to do this." Or "I should have done this by now." Or "I know I should be doing this already." And on and on. So, let me suggest that you let yourself off the hook. You've come into these pages to learn what you don't know. I doubt you'd scold a child for not knowing something they've never been taught. The same thing applies.

Let me share that I love my calendar system and the processes I have in place to stay super organized and get things done. But... I didn't know those systems until I *learned* them. Everything at which I excel now can be taught. I am not a special unicorn; I am just like you. Until I picked up a book, took an online course, or hired a coach, I didn't know what I was

> *Give yourself time and space to grow, and remember that you'll always be learning.*

doing. I struggled to get things done. I learned other systems – like you are about to do with this book – and I started implementing them and making them my own.

Like I said, I'm exactly like you. I still, at this moment in my life, want to get more done, too. I buy books and take courses, hoping I can find one tip or tool that will help me save an extra minute, hour, day, or week. And I have the same nervousness, thinking that I don't know how to achieve that next big goal... because I haven't done it yet. I have to learn it! It's simply part of the process, so please acknowledge that right now and rest assured that you are on the right path.

Okay, so you haven't done what you want to do or you still haven't taken any action toward achieving that big goal. Why not?

There are many different things that hold people back. Some of these same things may be holding you back right now. No matter what those things are or how many there may be, I want you to realize something very important: it's all in your head. No matter what the reason may be, it is simply a thought. Nothing more. A thought – that's it. Unfortunately, despite being nothing more than a thought, thoughts can become negatively powerful and subsequently drive certain actions that become our habits. You think something that causes you to experience a feeling, and that feeling causes you to act or react in a certain way, and with repetition, it creates a habit... and those habits start to dictate your life.

I have the privilege of working with some of the most incredible powerhouses in my Intentional Implementer™ program, but even high performers can struggle, and here are the most common issues.

Fears

Fear is what holds most people back. We're hard-wired to be afraid since in the very earliest days, fear was a real factor in staying alive. But if you want to get things done and achieve your big goals, it's time to get past your fears, and there are two fears that probably encompass all the others.

Fear of what others think. Those "others" can be family, friends, colleagues, even people from our past (like high school). It is a natural human instinct to want to be liked and to care about what other people think of us. We want to blend in more than we want to stand out. Taking big steps – bigger than those others are willing to take – can be scary because we worry about what they'll think. When we go after things our friends and family aren't pursuing, we start to stand out, and we worry about what they'll think and say.

We can hold onto the identity of who *they* think we are. You believe that if you switch things up, you'll become the talk of the town, the subject of gossip. "Did you know Susan is working for that new network marketing company. That's weird. Is it even a thing? I wonder why she left her other job." Or "Did you near that Annette launched a company and is going to work for herself. That's a big risk. I hope she knows what she's doing." Or "So I heard Jeff is writing a book. Can he even write?"

I'll share from experience that I struggled with that last one. That was definitely my fear. When I wrote my first book, my family didn't even find out about it until it was actually printed and in physical form. I was so nervous about what they'd think and say, so I didn't tell any of them. And here's the reality: my family was incredibly supportive when they found out. In looking back, that support would have made the process a bit easier. But I'd made up a story in my head – a thought – that took over as reality.

Unfortunately, if you're shaking your head, worried about what others may say, you're right. Someone might actually verbalize the thing you're afraid they'll say. People fear change, and when you decide to take action and start implementing, you are initiating change. In the accountability chapter, we're actually going to talk about who you are surrounding yourself with and what to say to family and friends when you begin accomplishing big things. And trust me, once you complete this book, you'll be well on your way to doing just that!

Fear of failure. Let's face it: the unknown is scary. We all like to stay within our personal comfort zones where we know exactly what it feels like and what to expect when we carry out a particular task. Take on something new, and it is scary, and our fear of the unknown rears up and makes us uneasy. Part of you isn't taking the action you need to take because you're nervous... afraid of what you don't know and afraid of what might happen.

We all like to be comfortable. Think about a cold morning in the dead of winter when you have to get out of bed and jump in the shower. The last thing you probably want to do is get undressed and wait for the water to heat up. You may even start to ask yourself, "Do I really need a shower today? How about just using some perfume? Would that work?"

> *"Everything you want is on the other side of fear."*
>
> *~ Jack Canfield*

In all likelihood, you put your discomfort aside and get in because you know you need to. Guess what? Just a few short minutes later, you probably don't want to get out! Think about the place you were standing not wanting to leave... and now you don't want to go back there. You're comfortable right where you are now. Yes, we like to be comfortable and we don't like to change from a state of comfort to one that makes us uncomfortable, uneasy, or downright scared.

Many people don't take the steps they need to because of their fear of failure. However, risking failure is a must if you want to take big steps. In fact, no great success was ever achieved without failure. Consider Edison's 10,000 or so attempts to create the light bulb. He's quoted as saying, "I have not failed. I've just found 10,000 ways that won't work." It's important to keep in mind that failure is not the opposite of success. Instead, it is a stepping stone toward it.

As we covered, you can't move forward unless you're learning new things, and you will not know how to do something new without trying and learning. You'll have many lessons to learn, and there will no doubt be many things that don't go your way. You will fail. However, that same failure is actually moving you closer to your goal (you now have experience and knowledge because of it), and it makes you stronger, more resilient, and more prepared for your *next* big goal.

Perfectionism

Gary Vaynerchuk, noted entrepreneur, posted this: "I want you to practice loving yourself and remember perfection is a mindset, a mindset that exposes insecurities and leads to unhappiness and lack of action.... Forget being perfect. Be you; it's better."

Oh boy, perfection can really hold you back! Although many people perceive me as a perfectionist, I could not *disagree* more. I actually see perfectionism as a negative quality. Why? It will slow you down and even bring you to a screeching halt more than anything. Perfection costs you so much valuable time when you are trying to make something "perfect." And here's the biggest issue: "perfect" is impossible.

In response, I always tell people, "I am not a perfectionist; I just have really high standards." I want you to not only reread that sentence – *I am not a perfectionist; I just have really high standards* – I want you to take it and own it! I want you to copy my motto. Say it with me now: I am not a perfectionist; I just have really high standards.

Here's why this sentence is so important: doing is learning. Something cannot truly be perfected, or "mastered" is my preferred word, until it is in action. When you take action and start doing, you will get feedback (as well as critical education and experience) faster than if you simply keep it to yourself and the item forever remains on your to-do list.

> *Don't waste time striving for perfection. It's impossible. Simply have high standards.*

We have a team of more than 50 employees in the two performing art academies I own, and it is impossible for us to see each other when most spend their time alone in their classrooms, so I make sure we schedule some fun social activities to actually talk and get to know each other better. Some of these activities have included dinners, casino nights (fake money, of course), a pedal tavern that involves riding a massive bike and bar hopping, and the latest was axe throwing. Now I've never thrown an axe before, and I'm sure I could have gone on the internet and found a million tips about hitting the bull's-eye. But only when you actually pick up the axe and throw it can you truly learn. Right? Trial and error… such a good teacher. So you throw the first one and realize, "Wow. That was awful. Let's not do it that way again." So you make an adjustment and get closer on the next throw, so you tweak again. Only when you've tried and learned will you be able to hit the bull's-eye!

So many people are spending – and wasting – far too much time "getting ready." They don't realize the best thing they could do is just jump in and start learning. In my example, pick up the axe and start throwing.

When I first started my consulting business, I did a lot of one-to-one coaching and prospects had to complete an application to work with me. In looking over applications that had been idle for six months to see if there were any leads that might be ready to commit, I came across one from a woman who I really liked and with whom I'd had a great conversation but who told me she wasn't ready. When I followed up previously, she said she was "getting ready to work with me, and as soon as I'm done getting ready, I'll reach out to schedule." When I checked out the link to her website six months later, it was broken. I didn't have the wrong link. She'd shut down the site because she'd shut down her business. Staying in the "getting ready" phase cost her the business. I truly believe if she would have started doing instead of worrying about getting or being ready, she would have moved forward faster. That doesn't guarantee that she would have been successful, but action would have given her feedback and saved time.

My advice to you right now is to immediately stop striving for perfection and "getting ready." It is time to start doing, so you start learning and acquiring the knowledge and experience you need. Knowledge is power, and it will point you in the right direction for taking the next step and how fast you'll move.

What's Your Why?

Some people don't take action because they don't want to achieve their goal badly enough. There's not enough reason behind it. Some entrepreneurs refer to the reason behind what they do as their "why." I call it "finding your fuel" – the reason you do what you do and why you want what you want. Your fuel is the catalyst that will take you where you really want to go. A quick word of caution: don't let your catalyst be shame, guilt, or fear, or you'll be headed away from what you truly want.

Perhaps you aren't implementing right now because you can't see a bigger picture. If that's the case, I say your why isn't big enough! For me, I ask myself what inaction and not moving forward will cost me, and I know I will regret *not* taking action far more than I will regret trying something new – and stumbling or failing outright – in going after what I want.

> **You need a big why and really strong fuel!**

Your why, your fuel, needs to be big enough to support that approach. When your fuel is weak, you will not be able to sustain progress and the work you are doing. Like an engine trying to run on watered down fuel, you'll sputter and stall.

When I work, I have a Post-it® note that is directly in my line of sight and it has three questions:

1. What would I like?
2. What would having that do for me?

3. Can I get there in a lighter, more fun way?

Question #2 is really critical. By asking it, we quickly realize that we do really want something and we'll discover we are really looking for an underlying reason. For example, let's say your answer to question #1 is that you want to lose 20 pounds. But what you really want is uncovered in the second question – to feel more energized. The third question is important to ask to ensure you are not trapping yourself into a single approach. There may be a more enjoyable path to get what you want.

Let me share my own example. I cut out sugar (for the most part), and someone asked me how I did it. It's not that I don't eat it, but it's definitely not part of my daily diet. It is sometimes a weekend treat. Now I love dessert and I could never have achieved sugar elimination if my reason was to lose weight. I would eat chocolate every day. Losing weight as my why wasn't big enough, and that fuel wasn't potent enough. If the goal was weight loss, I would rather keep the weight and eat the chocolate brownie. However, after witnessing my grandparents suffer from dementia and seeing the toll it took on the whole family for years, I started researching ways to lessen my own chances of a similar fate. Sugar consumption was partly to blame, and when I learned how sugar hurts our bodies in so many ways, my why became big enough to avoid eating it daily. It's not a matter of self-discipline. It is that my fuel is now stronger for why I don't eat it than why I'd want it.

I don't need will power or self-discipline because I want the outcome and result more than I want that activity. I want to be healthier more than I want the brownie. When your why is big enough and your fuel is strong enough, you don't have to worry about having enough will power. Your why is your driving power.

When people comment on how "disciplined" I am, it sounds like such a negative word, and it is. In its truest definition, it means using punishment to correct disobedience. Who wants that? Perhaps you're feeling discouraged, exhausted, and worn out with what's going on now, and that's driven by a belief that you don't have the will power or self-discipline, so it can't be done. In turn, why try? As we move through this book, I'm going to share a framework that can easily be followed, and when you do, you'll see how easy it really is, and people will be in awe of your will power. Start by getting clear about your why and ensure it's big enough. Once you have that in place, you'll find the self-discipline part comes easily.

What to Do Next?

Although it seems counterintuitive, your to-do list may actually be holding you back. You keep adding to it, thinking that's helping, but in reality, it becomes so crazy that you don't know where to start... so you don't. You stall and fail to implement and take any action at all. Maybe you wake up in the middle of the night with everything on your list swirling in your head. When you do get up, now feeling groggy and far from well-rested, you have no idea what to do first. We'll cover the best ways to prioritize, so you're ready to start your day on the right foot. When you learn that, you can stop worrying about the things that are happening tomorrow and go back to sleep. The middle of the night is not the right time to focus, and we'll talk about when to focus in an upcoming chapter.

Many times, I see entrepreneurs with unreasonable expectations. They think, "This should be easier. I should make money as soon as I open the doors and launch my business." They would never expect anyone to get done what they are doing, but for some reason, they put a ton of pressure on themselves to be faster, smarter, stronger, etc.

Hand in hand with this is impatience. I am the most impatient person – I don't want everything now... I wanted it all yesterday. That works for me and helps me move fast because of where I am in the journey. However, I don't want you to allow your impatience to make you quit because it is not happening fast enough. Remember, it's a learning process, and making progress right now is all that matters. If you stall because your expectations were unreasonable, it will take even longer. If you quit because of unreasonable expectations, you'll never get there at all. Yes, I want you to dream big and have a powerful why. I also want you to accept that achieving a big goal takes action and it also takes time.

Overthinking and obsessing also slow you down. We all have stories in our heads, and if we're not careful, those stories can become so engrained in our brains that we believe them and act in alignment with the false narrative we've created. I believe we can use this as an excuse for not doing anything. When you tell your brain all day and every day how busy you are and how you're never getting anything done, your actions start to prove your point. How is that helping? There is always a deeper meaning for why you aren't doing something, so be careful not to fall prey to the story in your head.

Be very careful about the thoughts in your head and let go of anything that isn't positive and moving you forward. Sometimes we get so fixated on something bad that's happened that we can't spend our time and energy on what we want to actually happen. This is where the law of attraction comes into play. What takes up your mental energy is what comes back to you. If all you think about is what you don't want, that is usually exactly what you end up with. But the good news is that the opposite is also true. Focus on what you do want, and you'll find it comes your way.

Additionally, don't dwell on your mistakes or that angry review someone posted online. Instead, think about

> *The law of attraction: Positive or negative thoughts bring positive or negative experiences and results.*

what you can learn from it, apply the lesson, and move on. Yes, I understand that's easier said than done, but remember that you are always learning, so mistakes are inevitable. Chalk up the experience so you can avoid repeating the mistake. Think about the last time you got stuck dwelling on something negative that happened and the length of time you spent stuck in that rut. Now think about how you could have better spent that time, focusing on the positive things you want to achieve. Don't let negative thinking steal your precious time.

Thinking Small

I'll be very honest with you: I've had this story in my head that "I'm small." And it's been hanging around in there for quite a while. I tend to think that others are always bigger, better, and smarter than I am. In turn, I think: "Why would they want to associate with me... have me speak on their stage... be interviewed on their podcast or be a guest on mine." You get the picture.

It was so engrained in my head, and the only way for me to move past it was to realize where it originated. I grew up going to a very small Christian school, and extracurricular activities outside of my school setting always involved the kids who attended public school. The only person I knew was my sister, and I always felt like we had to prove ourselves. We were the minority and were never part of the larger group who all knew each other and were friends. It happened a lot... and then it got worse. After grade school, we switched to the public high school, and I went from having ten kids in 8th grade to having 450 kids in 9th grade. I knew no one. Not one of my grade school classmates made the switch, and my sister was a grade younger, so even she wasn't there any longer. She's always been my sidekick, but now I was alone, feeling small and trying to prove myself and struggling to climb the ladder to make friends.

This scenario and my mental story – "I'm small and I'm not as good" – were not only holding me back, but it started to hold my team back as well. When my team would come to me with lofty ideas, I shut them down and told them "how reality really works." I always felt that others were on a much higher plateau than me. "They're way up here, and I'm down here, so they'd never find value in me and what I offer."

Let me share a story that gets right to the heart of this problem. I hired a new team member who, on her first day, said, "I'm going to get Suze Orman on the podcast."

My response: "No, no, no. You see this is how it works – I'm down here and Suze is way, way up here and she would never say yes." When I got off the team call, I recognized what I just did and saw that, wow, not only was my "I'm small" attitude affecting me, I was trying to bring everyone else down with me. I shot a message back to her: "If you want to reach out to her, go for it." She did, and guess what? I interviewed Suze Orman!

Getting Unstuck

Here's the framework that I used to get myself unstuck from the fake stories that were holding me back:

1. Recognize what is holding you back – aka, the fake story you tell yourself.

2. Uncover where that belief originated and talk through it with your adult perspective, not the child's perspective that started it.

3. Catch yourself when you're not taking action or taking the wrong action and ask if it's a result of your fake story. Talk to your younger self... as an adult! What would you say? If you find this difficult, pretend your child is telling you this story. What would you say to them in response?

4. Use that same advice for yourself. Go for the "ask" or take the action even if you don't feel ready because you will start to build your confidence. Now that I've interviewed Suze

Orman, I have a new level of confidence about the caliber of guests who will say yes to my show.

5. Leverage that spark of confidence to keep striving for more.

6. Make a gratitude highlights list. It's easy to forget what you've done and what you're capable of. I created a list of highlights for the year – those moments when I think, "Wow. I can't believe this just happened." Reviewing this list is incredibly powerful.

Keep a notebook to write out your thoughts. Journaling is a very powerful way to reveal the small thoughts that hold you back and remind yourself about all of your successes. I keep a blank journal in my office, and when I have a big task ahead or something that makes me nervous, I go through the framework above and write it all down. As I start to write, things come up that I didn't know were there. The next time you're facing something similar, I want you to pull out your notebook and just start writing down what is in your head. Things you don't even realize are there will magically appear on the page.

Working through this will help you realize that you don't need your "small" thought to hold you back any longer!

Start Unlocking and Implementing

- First, admit that you are the only thing holding you back.

- Accept that you have to learn and don't scold yourself for failing at something you were never taught.
- Whatever is holding you back is in your head... nothing more than a thought.
- Fears – that of what others will think and say and of failure – can derail your efforts to achieve what you want. Risking failure is a must if you want to take big steps, and stop worrying about what others think.
- Copy and own my motto: I am not a perfectionist; I just have really high standards.
- Stop striving for perfection and "getting ready" and start doing instead.
- Your fuel is the reason you do what you do and want what you want. Be sure your fuel is strong and potent.
- Don't allow yourself to quit because of your impatience when things don't seem to be happening fast enough. Give yourself time to learn.
- Remember the law of attraction: What takes up your mental energy is what comes back to you.
- Stop thinking you're smaller or less important than anyone else.
- Follow my framework to get unstuck from the thoughts in your head.

Get even more helpful information to unlock yourself from whatever it is that is holding you back inside our companion course at:
www.implementationcode.co/freecourse

What's Holding You Back?

Chapter Two:

Start Small... or Be Doomed

It's not about a drastic change in your life. It's about committing to a one percent – yes, just one percent – increase in any area of your life that you want to improve. I want to talk about deciding and committing... how small incremental habits can drastically change your outcomes.

I want to achieve big things, and I know you do too. In fact, my goals are usually so massive that the first time I write them down, I do a double take. I can't believe I just wrote that. (And yes, writing them matters and I will teach you how to organize the chaos of your one billion goals.) Maybe you have goals that you haven't told anyone because they are so lofty, you're worried about what other people will think or say. (There's that fear that's holding you back.)

So let's dive into the power of starting small. Now please be very clear: I am not saying be small, think small, or play small. I'm saying start small and give yourself little tasks or things to get started that will make the whole process feel lighter, easier, and less overwhelming. For example, writing this book was a big undertaking, and the idea of sitting down and writing the whole thing was almost too much to imagine. So I started by creating the title and the chapter titles. Then I jotted down what I wanted to cover in each chapter – not so much a formal outline as simply my thoughts. After that, I jumped in and wrote the introduction and expanded on my thoughts for each chapter. Then it was on to the book, paragraph by paragraph, section by section, and chapter by chapter. This massive project became a series of small, very achievable steps.

Taking on any massive project can stop you before you even get started if you stay too focused on the big picture. If I only focused on writing an entire book, I'm certain writer's block would have kept the page blank. When you are feeling overwhelmed, break down any project – massive or even not so massive – into smaller components and focus on those. Take it one step, one paragraph, one page at a time. The first step gets the ball rolling and starts building your momentum and forward progress.

> *"We can't become what we need to be by remaining what we are."*
>
> *~ Oprah Winfrey*

We must change our behavior if we want to achieve a new outcome. Start small for quick wins and fast results. Little wins are still wins, and they help you learn, gain confidence, and keep you moving in the right direction. Incorporating new habits can be difficult because it is manual. It's easier to build any habit when you start small. Yes, you have to work and practice new habits (and smaller components of new habits), but the more you repeat the process, the more automated it becomes.

In terms of getting in better shape, you can't just decide to run a marathon, or even a mile for that matter. You'll have success when you start small. "I'll walk for ten minutes today." Repeat that small step, and you'll find yourself automatically doing it and then you can build on it, increasing to 15 minutes, 30 minutes, and then perhaps running instead of walking. Pretty soon, you don't stop to think about exercising or working out in the morning. You hear the alarm go off, and without even thinking about it, you suddenly realize you're in your workout clothes and heading out the door.

Four Phases of Achievement

There is a four-step process or four phases that you need to go through in order to achieve any goal.

Learn. Learning is phase one. No physicist can carry out complex calculations without first learning the basics. The equation $E = mc^2$ would never have been possible without $1+1=2$ as a starting point. To achieve any goal, you have to learn the basics first.

Remember my earlier story about taking my team on an axe-throwing outing? My friends were not at all surprised that I researched tips on throwing an axe online before the event. (I know, complete nerd and clearly competitive.) Whatever you want to do, there are almost always people who have gone before you with wisdom to share – whether that's throwing an axe trying to hit the bull's-eye or developing a marketing campaign to improve your company's brand and recognition. Be open to learning and remember that learning is a lifelong endeavor.

Do. Phase two is all about doing the work. Phase two is messy and is not the final step. Failure to do is what derails any goal or ambition; however, there's a really common misconception I see with many clients with whom I work. They think that if they learn everything they can, they'll be successful. I've had people tell me, "I've spent enough time and money learning. Now it's time I get results." The problem is they haven't engaged in the "do" part. You haven't earned anything and you don't deserve anything until you put in the time doing the work.

Don't forget that when you first start to "do," you will most likely fail a few times. Like I said, phase two is messy. Intellectual knowledge is one thing, but applied knowledge – that which you get by doing, aka experience – is what generates results. I did all the research I could find about axe throwing, but until I picked it up, felt its weight, and acclimated to how it felt in my hand, I only had intellectual knowledge about it. I gained a lot of applied knowledge after hurling it a few times.

Yes, research and learning are critical, but don't expect to be amazing right out of the gate. You are going to make mistakes in converting your intellectual knowledge into real experience.

Refine. Once you've gained some experience, it's time to continue to tweak and refine your actions to generate better, faster, and more effective results. In the case of my axe-throwing example, I learned that when I choked up on the handle a bit, I gained a lot more control. That was my "refine" stage in my quest to hit the bull's-eye.

Keep refining until you find your groove and your sweet spot in which all of your efforts run, more or less, on autopilot. Phase three can be tweaked forever, but you will reach a point at which you are good enough and you have to be okay with that. The perfectionist in you will want to keep tweaking – keep improving – and yes, we always want to continue to beat our last result, but it no longer becomes our number one priority. We have to let it go and move on to phase four.

Maintain. Once you've established your habit or activity and feel good about where it's at, you are going to have to check in regularly to ensure that you aren't losing the ground you gained. For example, if your goal was to lose 20 pounds and you did, you'll need to regularly step on the scale to ensure you are maintaining your desired weight. This isn't as difficult as the learn and do phases, but it still takes a bit of effort and is a critical component to the end result and success. Without continuing to step on the scale, it's very easy to wake up and realize those 20 pounds are back.

When you're in maintenance mode with any habit, it's a lot like changing the oil in your car. If you fail to do so, your car stops running smoothly and ultimately stops running altogether. Enter the little check engine light. Yes, it's annoying when it pops on and starts flashing at you, but it's a handy reminder to take your car for an oil change. In the same way, you need to build in triggers or reminders for checking in on your habits and what you've achieved. It's your own personal check engine light. It could be a calendar reminder to step on the scale.

> *Without maintenance, things have a way of "reverting to previous state."*

Setting the goal is only the first step. You have to put habits and maintenance triggers in place to make sure it happens, and once it does, to ensure it doesn't "revert to former state."

Habit Forming

The key to developing any habit is to start small. If you haven't worked out in months, jumping in with five days a week of vigorous activity is not a good starting point and will not be sustainable. Let's face it, after day one, you'll be stiff and sore, quite possibly too stiff and sore to work out on day two. By day two, your goal of getting in shape is out the window.

I had a similar experience. I knew I had to get an earlier start on the day to get more done. I'd been waking up around 7:00 at the same time as my children. I wanted to start waking up at 5:00 to gain two additional hours, but I knew trying to do this at once would not be an easy, lighter, or fun approach. Cold turkey tactics rarely are. Instead, I started going to bed 15 minutes earlier and then waking up 15 minutes earlier. When that felt normal to me, I again shifted by another 15 minutes over and over until I was right where I was aiming for: 5:00 a.m. start without feeling groggy and sleepy.

The first day I woke at 6:45 was a small win, and small wins always help you gain momentum. More importantly small wins boost your confidence, and confidence is the key ingredient to help you continue to implement. With small wins, you will create long-term habits that are here to stay. Don't think small, but start small!

There are studies I've seen (and you've probably seen the same ones) that suggest that you must repeat something for 21 days, or some other magic number, for it to become a habit. Now that may be true, but habits can also get lost and that can happen very quickly. In my case, I grew up as a dancer, so I didn't have to work out. Dancing provided the exercise I needed. Eventually, I stopped dancing and then even stopped teaching dance. It seemed all of a sudden, I was at a bowling alley instead, eating fries and drinking beer. One of my friends shared that she'd heard through the grapevine that I was "getting chubby." I swear to you: I dropped the French fry from my fingers back into the little red basket, shoved the beer away from me, and ordered water. I had no idea I'd gained 20 pounds.

Since then, I've been in plenty of different workout programs like CrossFit and have had several gym memberships, but working out always felt like a chore, so I didn't keep up with it. I had zero accountability, so I hired a trainer. After two years of working out three times a week, I really started to enjoy it, and it was truly an ingrained habit. I no longer needed the trainer and was working out every day on my own. I'd formed a habit and was excited to continue with it.

Sounds good, right? Well, like I said, habits can easily get lost. After flying home from a speaking engagement, I'd caught a bug on the plane and was really sick for about two weeks. Then I was off to another speaking engagement, followed by a four-day business conference that ran 12 hours each day. No time to work out. Before I knew it, 30 days had gone by without me working out one time. Getting back into a workout routine after so much time off was very, very difficult. I was starting from scratch.

> *Even the good habits you've created can quickly derail. When it happens, start small when you start over.*

So how'd I do it? I started small. My first goal was to work out easy three days a week. Then onto four days, and finally back to five days. I'm sharing this story because I don't want you to think that after repeating something for 21 days and forming a habit means that it will automatically stick... no matter how long you've been doing it. It's really easy to get thrown off track, despite your best intentions.

Beware that an "all or nothing" attitude will kill your goals. For example, let's say you decide to stop watching TV for 4.5 hours a day (the American average), and you stop cold turkey. Then your friend invites you over for the premiere of your all-time favorite show, and you agree. Since you've already broken the habit for an hour, suddenly you cave and revert back to your old 4.5 hours a day. There is a phrase that, when it comes to habits, is a game changer if you eliminate it from your vocabulary. Ready for it? "I'll start again on Monday."

Think about this: You've decided on a new goal or priority in your life that's important to you. Oh, but it's the weekend or it's even Thursday with the weekend looming large, so you feel it will be best to start fresh on Monday. If you've found yourself in this pattern, my question to you is: Why are you delaying your priorities? I don't care what you did today. Get back on track now. In another relatable example, you've made your health a priority and have been doing well with the foods you eat. Then you have a greasy cheeseburger for lunch, so you figure the rest of the day is shot, so you have

> *"All or nothing" is a goal killer!*

sugary snacks in the afternoon and make poor choices at dinner along with a decadent dessert.

I am sorry my friend, but that attitude and approach are sabotaging everything you hope to gain. Don't justify that you might as well ruin your priority for the rest of the day... or for three days if you think you're better off starting on Monday. The truth is you are better starting off right now and getting back on track immediately. Okay, you ate the cheeseburger. Salad for dinner and move forward again aligning with your priorities.

The "all or nothing" attitude will always undermine what you are trying to achieve, so drop it, and stop justifying the nonsense going on in your head. I believe you can do anything, but your actions have to show that *you* believe you can do anything and are willing to work for it. Instead of "all or nothing," starting small gives you quick wins and helps you establish your belief that you can do this. Your confidence goes up, and when your belief in yourself grows, your goals grow, too.

Get Realistic and Start Small

When starting small, you have to ensure you give yourself enough time to create and implement what you want to accomplish. So many times I see people trying to replicate what someone else did with half the experience, one-quarter of the prep time, and one-eighth of the effort... and they expect the same result. That is never going to happen. Get realistic.

Here's the framework to follow to start small in forming a new habit:

1. Decide what you want (e.g., drink eight glasses of water a day). If you're unsure about what you should choose, don't worry. In the next chapter, we'll cover prioritizing the million things in your head. I have a million things, too, but one at a time. Remember, we're starting small and not finishing everything today. Keep it simple for now.

2. Get the resources you need to make it happen. In our example, I probably have everything I need, but I can make it simple by finding two 32-ounce water bottles and filling them. That way, I don't have to keep track and only need to drink both during the course of the day. Sometimes, your goal will require you to purchase something (e.g., water bottles, healthy groceries, weight set, etc.).

3. With your supplies in hand, create a trigger. Triggers are critical to successful habit formation. Make your goal visible as a reminder. Post a note where you'll see it first thing every morning. This is your trigger. Your mind will not remind you because you are forming a new habit and are out of your norm. Here are a few other trigger ideas:

   - Set a phone alarm. If you want to work out at 6:30, set a reminder alarm for 6:20.
   - If you have a calendar system that you use consistently, add a recurring time to focus on your selected activity. If you aren't already in the habit of using a calendar, obviously this won't work because it

won't trigger you – you'll never see it. And if you're not currently using an online calendar, I'll hopefully soon convince you how it can change your life along with a few tricks in my free companion course at: www.implementationcode.co/freecourse.

- Backup triggers: Yes, you need a backup in case your first trigger doesn't work. Maybe you want to read a book a week and add that to your calendar for every Friday. A good backup trigger would be to set a date about 90 days out to check your progress. For me, I love learning and attending conferences but leave with information overload and can only start on one idea but have 57 pages of notes. I start on the first idea and make a note in 30 or 60 days to review my conference notes to implement the next idea. Too many people leave conferences and workshops with plenty of notes but without a trigger system to continue to implement the great ideas they've learned, so their notebooks gather dust and all momentum is lost.

4. Track your progress. Actually make yourself a check list and physically check off a box when you complete your task each day. Your brain gets a dopamine hit when you check off or cross off something from your list, so you'll want to

continue to do it. I know this sounds silly, but I highly recommend using a physical pen and paper when creating and tracking a new habit. Because it's physical, you will more likely see it than if it is hidden somewhere in your phone or computer. (Inside our companion course, we have a free implementation tracker. Go to: www.implementationcode.co/freecourse to download yours.)

Once you get started and the more often you repeat your desired habit, it will become a natural part of your day. You'll immediately fill up your two water bottles and start your day without thinking about it. I start every day with a big cup of water. My body now tells me I need it, and I no longer need a reminder or trigger; however, that wasn't always the case.

Keep tracking your progress. Remember: we can control the effort but not the result. I can control that I'll wake up and work out five days a week, but I can't directly control how much weight I'll lose. I keep tracking and tweaking and experimenting with my efforts so that I ultimately get the results I want.

The most important thing when starting a new habit is to pick one. Never try to start ten new things at once. Keep it small; keep it to one. It is going to take some brain power to create a single new habit, so don't go overboard. This chapter has its name for a reason. If you don't start small, you'll be doomed to fail. Get your small quick wins, build momentum, and keep going!

Start Unlocking and Implementing

- Don't think or play small, but start small... always.
- Small starts lead to quick wins and fast results that build momentum.
- Remember the four-step process: Learn. Do. Refine. Maintain.
- Regardless of the number of days it may take to create a habit, they can get lost quickly... even those habits that you may have been doing for years.
- Lose the "all or nothing" attitude. It will kill your goals.
- Stop delaying. Today and now are always the best times to get started.
- Follow the framework to start small and successfully create a new habit.
- Continue to track your progress and set reminders to check in 30, 60, or 90 days from now.

Start small, but *get started* with our companion course at: www.implementationcode.co/freecourse

Start Small... or Be Doomed

Chapter Three:

Hyper-Focus – Like a Laser Beam

My daughter asked for a telescope for her seventh birthday, and she was "over the moon" when she unwrapped it. So much so that she wanted to try it immediately. With nightfall still hours away, we placed it by the window, so she could start exploring with it.

In a very short time, she yelled out, "I'm not finding anything!"

So I asked, "Well, what are you looking for?"

Her reply was a shrug.

My husband pointed to a bridge in the distance and said, "Let's find that." Within seconds, she was able to get it in focus, and to her delight, she could see both cars and pedestrians crossing the bridge.

I often find my clients have a similar problem. They can't get anything in focus because they're unsure what they should be looking for. It's so much easier to hit your goals when you know exactly what you should be aiming for, shooting at, and focusing on.

When entrepreneurs are in motion, they think they are doing what they should be doing to grow their businesses and ultimately boost their bottom lines. However, they are confusing busyness with productivity. Trust me, you can be busy all day without making a difference. So what does it mean to be productive? Look closely at the word, consider its origin, and notice "produce" in there. Productivity is about **producing** results. You can be busy all day long without generating meaningful results. There is a clear difference between busyness and productivity, so we're going to take this chapter to figure out what you should be producing, so you can laser in and get hyper-focused.

365 vs. 90

Goal setting has been one of my secret weapons for a long time. From the time I was 21 until about 30, I always set annual goals. It worked well enough. I didn't have any complaints about my progress and often hit the goals I'd set. However, when I discovered 90-day goals, it was a complete game changer. Annual goals don't create any sense of urgency. Quite the opposite. I realized I had all year to accomplish them, so I moved at a slower pace. When I started setting 90-day goals, I quickly learned that I needed to get in gear and immediately start getting things done if I was going to achieve my goal.

A year is a long time, and many things can change during that time. Those changes (that may or may not be within your control) can make an annual goal irrelevant or even meaningless. On the other hand, 90 days isn't too long. There's a foreseeable deadline to get you moving toward achievement. At the same time, 90 days isn't too short, either. It's far enough in the future to tackle a reasonably sized goal and still be achievable. Plus, that time frame allows for a quick re-set when needed. If you're going to fail, you fail fast and can correct and move forward again. It's also the right length of time for which to be hyper-

> *90-day goals help you expedite results and success.*

focused, especially when you have several goals. Focus on three and 90 days later, evaluate your progress before setting new ones.

I call these my "Quarterly Master 3" goals. Every quarter, I write these on a Post-it® where I can see it every day – in fact, on the wall right in front of me. I make the goals short and sweet and itemize them in their order of importance. I place the date at the top, so on January 1st, I write "April 1" at the top. I have 90 days to achieve these three goals.

Like my daughter with her telescope, if you don't know what to look for and focus on, you won't see what you want to see. If you don't know what you're shooting for, you won't be happy with your results. If you want to implement more than you ever have, getting hyper-focused on what you want will be your saving grace.

But What If...

Before we dive in, I want to address the reader who doesn't know what they want to do. Even if this doesn't sound like you, I want you to keep reading anyway. Why? Because at some stage in your life, you are going to find yourself in this situation – not sure what to do. You will have moments when you're at a stage of "I don't like my life, but I'm not sure what to do next." And there will be times of the opposite feeling when life is so great that you don't know what to possibly put on your vision board next. As someone who's set goals for almost two decades, I assure you that I go through both stages at varying times.

In my early 20s, I had a top ten list. It felt like a bucket list of things I wanted to do over my lifetime. The worst part? By age 29, I had achieved them all. Now you may be thinking, "Boo hoo, Stacy. It must be nice to achieve everything you want by that age."

However, even as a high achiever (like you might be right now), it landed me at a place of feeling lost, unmotivated, and unchallenged – like I'd already peaked and I hated that feeling. I was stuck. The real moral of my story is that I got through it and have faced it again since at various times. So whether you're struggling right now or if you hit this stage in the future, here are three tips to get unstuck.

Tip #1: Keep moving. Continue to take action even if you aren't sure what you're doing or why. All too often, I have clients repeatedly tell me they're "stuck."

> *Even the highest achievers get stuck once in a while. When it happens, keep moving.*

They say the word over and over. I give them a strategy to try, and a week later the response I get is, "It was a good strategy, but I'm stuck and I'm not quite sure if that would work for me."

My response, should I be able to jump through my computer monitor (most of my coaching is done virtually) would be to grab their cute little face, shake them, and shout, "Just do *something* and you won't be stuck!"

Picture a car stuck in the mud. Wheels are spinning and dirt is flying. The driver rocks it back and forth trying to gain traction. That may work. If not, they'll have to take more drastic action like getting other folks to help push or even calling a tow truck. The point is, they're taking action; they're doing something. They're not just sitting behind the steering wheel hoping the car will magically become unstuck without them doing a thing.

This is exactly what those people who repeatedly complain about being stuck do. They're sitting in the mud, not attempting to move, refusing help from those driving by and offering suggestions that may help the situation. They turn them down and effectively say, "That's okay. I'm stuck but I'm going to continue to complain about it, and I'm going to tell you about my problem of being stuck every time you drive past me."

Friends, let me be very clear: no one wants to be around that person. Like your broke friend who keeps *talking* about not having enough money. The one who keeps *talking* about being overweight. The one who keeps *talking* about the horrible relationship she's in. You know what I mean. They're like the driver sitting in the car hoping it magically becomes unstuck. The people around you don't want to hear your same complaint over and over when you aren't doing anything to get yourself out of the situation.

It's different if you are actively *working* toward something better. People see your drive and they want to help... but only to help those who are doing something – taking some action – to get out of the mud and unstuck.

Keep trying, keep moving, keep doing anything until something starts to work and you start to gain traction. Yes, there are times when I feel stuck, and when that happens, I like to get out of my normal routine and do something different from the regular, day-to-day stuff. Pick up a new book, go to a conference or workshop, meet new people, learn from a new mentor, spice it up a little bit. You will never get different results when you do the same thing every day.

Tip #2: Watch your language when getting unstuck. First, remove the word "stuck" from your vocabulary. Replace "I'm stuck" with "I'm committed to figuring out the next chapter in my life or the next action to take." Your words have a big impact. In fact, they're everything.

First, with words you are telling your brain, "I'm stuck" and it becomes a self-fulfilling prophecy. Second, you affect those around you with your words. When we publicly talk about what we don't like, even negative comments about ourselves, it affects others in the room. Imagine complaining about being overweight when someone in the room is even heavier. How do you think you're making that person feel? I have a friend who suggests dinner and forewarns me how disgusting she looks – in workout clothes, hair is a mess, no makeup, etc. And she shows up looking like she was a model in a photo shoot for Nike. Now I feel disgusting!

> *Words matter. Always monitor what comes out of your mouth whether you say it to yourself or someone else.*

Negative talk helps no one and is especially detrimental when done in front of your kids. You are truly setting the worst possible example. If you're in this habit, it probably dates back to your own childhood. Please, stop the negative language!

Tip #3: Get inspired and model those who have what you want. The days of jealousy are over. Why? Because you don't need to be jealous. You can have what everyone else has. Everything can be taught. You have to decide that you are teachable. When I say model someone you aspire to be, I mean everything – when they sleep, get up, what they eat, how they work out, what they read, what they do for fun… how hard they work!

The life we build is the result of the actions we take. If you want someone's life, start acting like that person would act. If you want a bigger house, want your kids to attend a certain school, want to take a long overdue vacation, what actions do you need to take? Find your model.

Keep these tips in your back pocket and pull them out when you start to feel stuck, so you can quickly get back in the groove and keep moving forward.

Creating Your Quarterly Master 3 Goals

When determining your Quarterly Master 3 goals, I want you to ask yourself three questions… and they're going to sound familiar:

1. What would I like?
2. What would having that do for me?
3. Can I get there in a lighter, more fun way?

As you'll recall, these were the questions I wanted you ask when you were determining your big why. Your goals and your why must work in tandem.

Write down what comes to mind and refrain from going beyond three and listing four, five, six, and seven… thinking you'll actually achieve more. Nope. Three only. Why? Remember that you have to start small. It's the best way to stay in control and avoid becoming overwhelmed. Also, when your list looks too long, it becomes paralyzing and you stop moving. We certainly don't want that!

If I looked at your calendar, would it reflect your Quarterly Master 3? Honestly, when I do calendar audits with my Intentional Implementer™ clients, their goals are anything but clear on their calendar. The best tip I can share is to allot time to accomplish the tasks that support your three goals before lunch. In fact, reserve the entire morning for them. Imagine blocking out 9:00 a.m. until noon every day to work on your goals. It's easy to see how things would get done!

Now, let's say you're not a business owner. You're working full time for someone else and have a side hustle, so you think this isn't going to work. It can, and the strategy has two parts. First, make sure working on your goals comes before anything else, and second, allot half of your available hours to them. When I was building my business, I was going to school and working another job, so there

> *Make your priorities come first on your schedule, and when you want it badly enough, you'll find time.*

seemed to be no extra time, but I made the time. Get up earlier to work on your goals before anything else on your schedule. Being hyper-focused is critical and we'll cover that more in-depth shortly.

Figure out when you are able to dedicate your time and put it on your calendar. If it's not on your schedule, it won't happen. These are actually appointments with your goals. Don't cancel on them. Just like you wouldn't blow off a friend or colleague, treat yourself and your goals with the same respect. If you commit to working on your goals on Saturday morning and someone invites you to breakfast, say,

"I actually have an appointment, but how about lunch?" Got it? Make sense?

This is when we find out who really wants it. Are you going to make the time or make excuses about why you are busy? When someone tells me they're busy, I almost always see that I'm accomplishing more and have more on my plate, yet they can't find the time. The problem is simple – their why is not big enough; their fuel is not strong enough. I can't want your dreams more than you do. It doesn't work that way. You have to want it and you have to want it more than anything else.

Zeroing In

So with that said, it's time to zero in, and here are four steps for staying hyper-focused.

Laser Beam Step #1: Make a decision and commit. The worst place to be is sitting on the fence. If you find yourself there or trying to decide which road to take, ask yourself the following questions, and I highly recommend you write the answers in your journal. When you actually write, you might be surprised about what comes out as your answer:

1. What worries you about making this decision?
2. What does your gut say?
3. What is the biggest reason you don't want to do this?
4. What is the biggest reason you want to do this?
5. Would you have more regret doing it or not doing it?

6. What is your indecisiveness costing you?
7. What could this decision mean for you?
8. What are three pros that could come from making this decision?
9. What would need to happen in order for you to make a decision?
10. What would the person you most admire do?

Laser Beam Step #2: Be selective. Say yes to the things that move you closer to achieving your Quarterly Master 3 goals... and no to everything else! I know a lot of people struggle to say no. They want to be "nice" or they say yes under pressure when they really want to say no. It is time to be selfish. It is time to check on your priorities, not someone else's.

In business, we develop our "ideal client" – the one who is perfect for us to attract and work with. I want you to apply this same thinking in all areas of your life, but instead of the ideal client, we'll call it the "ideal yes." For example, when you are asked to volunteer for something, what would an ideal yes look like? Does it depend on the time involved, the schedule, the people, the mission? When you know in advance which situations are a yes – or a no – it is much easier to stick to the boundaries you set.

Let's say I'm asked to volunteer at my kid's school. First, they are looking for two parent volunteer chaperones. I know I will barely see my own child during the event, so for me, it's not an ideal yes. Later, they invite parents to attend school to watch the classroom activities during which time I could spend the entire day with my child. That's an ideal yes for me.

As another example: I'm a podcaster and am often invited to be on others' podcasts. It's a great way for me to advertise my own podcast, so I want to say yes as often as possible. However, new podcasters are popping up all the time, and they quickly realize that it's not as easy as it seems and may quit before they air any episodes.

> *When you're clear about your "ideal yes," it is easy to maintain boundaries.*

Because of that, agreeing to an interview is no longer an automatic ideal yes for me. Now I've honed my criteria to make it a yes: the podcast must be six-months-old, consistently releasing weekly episodes, and have at least 50 reviews. These factors indicate to me that the podcaster is serious about what they do. When the interview invitation meets those criteria, it's an ideal yes for me. If not, it's easy for me to stick to my boundaries so I don't waste my time.

Take time right now to write down the various things you are asked to do or have to do for your business or career. Then, next to each, write down what would be an ideal yes for each. Get really clear on what that looks like and ensure it is worth your time!

And get a free download on creating your ideal yes: www.implementationcode.co/freecourse

Laser Beam Step #3: Say goodbye to multitasking and stay in the zone. You may believe that you're being more productive when multitasking – switching from one task to another, performing two tasks at once, or performing tasks in rapid succession. I'll tell you you're wrong, and it's not just me saying that. According to *Business News Daily*, "A 2009 Stanford University study from Clifford Nass found that heavy multitaskers were less mentally organized, struggled at switching from one task to another, and had a hard time differentiating relevant from irrelevant details." And that study is only one of many that support the productivity killer that is multitasking.

Our brains aren't designed to multitask, and it takes time to switch gears when you are switching tasks. Smart phones and the inundation of media and messages we all face every day may make us think we're being more productive, but the truth is that we're not only less productive, the work we do produce is often sloppy and of poor quality.

It's physically impossible to focus on more than one thing at a time. If I tell you to picture yellow butterflies, your mind immediately goes there, and you drop whatever else you were thinking about. You have forgotten what you were thinking about and now you have to take time to recall it. Very unproductive.

Switch tasking is equally unproductive. Imagine you have your inbox open and you receive an email requesting a payment. You click the link to the service provider to make the payment and you're distracted by an ad that pops up. Before you know it, you're out shopping on Amazon as a result of the ad. Then you remember that you originally opened the email to make a payment, so you go back to it. This is not productive, and there is no efficiency in this behavior.

Immerse yourself in the task at hand and don't switch to the next one until you are done. If you worry about forgetting, simply pull out a note sheet and write, "Pay Sally." Problem solved.

Laser Beam Step #4: Create a vision board. Your Quarterly Master 3 goals represent what you want to do; your vision board shows **why** you want to do it. In my case, a Quarterly Master 3 might be "20 new members in my Intentional Implementer™ mastery program"; however, my vision board depicts a tropical vacation and my dream home.

When you look at your goals and don't feel very excited to take action, look at your vision board about why you want to reach the goal and refuel yourself to get moving. Additionally, your vision board keeps you focused on what you want. We already covered the law of attraction, focusing on what you want rather than on what you don't want, and I've had some crazy things become reality for me as a result of my vision board.

Years ago, I wanted to open a second performing arts academy location, so I started looking for something to represent that on my vision board. I went online and found a place for rent that would be a good fit for my studio – great location, good size, and it would work perfectly for us. I printed the picture and placed it on my vision board. It was on the wall for a while and then packed up when we moved. Years later, after we'd settled into our new house, we came across boxes that hadn't been unpacked. (Ever been there?) In one of those boxes was my vision board. I hadn't seen it in years and had forgotten about this one. The crazy part is that it was the exact building and exact suite that we'd acquired years later! I completely forgot that that image represented my goal. That's just one of many that have come to fruition.

Don't think things magically appear or happen because you post them on your vision board. However, seeing it every day helps fuel your actions toward achievement and results. In the case of my photo, I believe that some part of my brain, even subconsciously, remembered it. I was also very specific in my choice before I added it to my vision board. Choose your images wisely and see them every day.

Start Unlocking and Implementing

- If you aren't sure what you're looking for, nothing comes into focus.
- Annual goals are nice, but 90-day goals will get you faster results.
- Create your Quarterly Master 3 goals and keep it to three.
- Even if you are a high achiever, there will be times when you feel stuck. Ask:
  - What would I like?
  - What would having that do for me?
  - Can I get there in a lighter, more fun way?
- Keep moving; watch your language; model those who have what you want.
- Schedule time for your goals and priorities on your calendar and stick to it.
- Follow the laser-beam tips to get more done: Commit and get off the fence; create your ideal yes; stop multitasking; and create your vision board.

To really get and stay hyper-focused, check out our companion course at:
www.implementationcode.co/freecourse

Chapter Four

Prioritizing: Get It Right from the Start

"The key is not to prioritize what's on your schedule but to schedule your priorities."
~ Stephen Covey, author and speaker

So let me ask you: Would there ever be a situation that would cause you to miss your child's high school graduation? Most will respond with an emphatic "No way!" I wouldn't miss it for the world. But let me now add to the situation: Your other child was in a serious car accident and has been airlifted to the hospital. That changes things, does it not? Why? Because your priority has shifted.

Priorities shift all the time, even if they are not once-in-a-lifetime or life-threatening. Every day, we choose what is most important in that moment. Whether or not it is really a priority or important, you are making it a priority by getting it done now. If I looked at your calendar right now, would I be able to tell what your priorities are? Sure, it's easy to say something is a priority, but our actions don't always align with our words.

Prioritizing correctly is critical to not just getting things done, but getting the important things done – the things that will get you the results you really want. Get ready. This is a big chapter. This is where we'll start to figure out what to do first. Prioritizing your goals and dreams is critical to combat the sense of overwhelm that often occurs. If you've ever thought or said, "My to-do list is so big I just don't know where to even start," this chapter has you covered. Let's jump right in.

Brain Dump

Merriam Webster defines a brain dump as "the act or an instance of comprehensively and uncritically expressing and recording one's thoughts and ideas (as on a particular topic)."

Your brain isn't really meant to store information. Its primary function is to process information. Getting all of your to do's out of your head (aka a brain dump) is the best thing you can do, but of course, not every idea is worth keeping or even writing down. Some of your ideas aren't important and they may not even be any good. How do I determine what ideas aren't worth keeping? They're the ones that automatically get pushed down the list for days, weeks, or even months until I eventually look at it and say, "I'm getting rid of it!"

So, it's time to do a brain dump. Get a piece of paper or your journal, sit down, and write all of your thoughts about what needs to be done. During your initial brain dump, you'll be trying to remember everything. That's okay. Get it all on paper. Then get ready to freak out.

> *Your brain is much better at processing than remembering. Use your brain effectively.*

The problem with brain dumping is that when you see everything you have to do, it's almost a given that you'll feel overwhelmed because that sheet of paper represents about 62 hours of work to be done in a 24-hour day... and yeah, you'd like to get at least a little sleep too.

I understand that it's overwhelming, but what's even scarier to me is that for all of these things now on your paper, previously your only reminder was your brain. I'm actually terrified for you. Despite the human brain being an incredible computer, there is no way you are going to be able to remember everything.

Bear with me as you start to brain dump and feel overwhelmed. It's like cleaning out your closet – the kind of cleaning when you take everything out (everything!) and it looks crazy messy in the room. You wonder how you ever accumulated it all, but now that it's out, you sort through item by item, deciding what to toss, what to donate, and what to keep. And once you put those "keep" items back, you have much more space and it looks organized. You can find things quickly. You're glad you tackled it.

That is what brain dumping combined with my priority framework is going to do for you. There are two ways to approach this. You can download my free priority sheet at www.implementationcode.co/freecourse or grab a notebook. The download includes all of the step-by-step instructions, so if you opted to simply use a notebook, here's what to do:

Start writing down all of the things you know you need to get done like:
- Schedule a dental appointment
- Cancel massage membership
- Create a job posting for a new hire
- PJ day at school is next Tuesday
- Sign the vendor contract

- Stop by the bank to update the account
- Make a deposit while at the bank
- … you get the idea: everything!

It doesn't matter if it's business or personal or whatever else you have going on. I'm all about having one to-do list, one calendar, one email inbox. The simpler we make it, the easier it is.

Look over your brain dump and start to incorporate the items into your schedule. Once you do this initial brain dump, you'll find brain dumps happen all the time – because they're helpful and keep your mind clearer. You'll start doing them without thinking about it. In fact, the second a thought pops into my head now, I immediately get it into tangible form and out of my head, so I'm not relying on my brain as a reminder. If I'm in the office, I jot it on the notepad I keep by my desk. If I'm on the road or at the grocery store, I send an email to myself. Why an email? Because I am sure to see it later. If I make a note somewhere else in my phone, there is no reminder for me to go back and check it later. Without a trigger, it's lost.

You know how your computer, tablet, or phone all run more smoothly after a reboot and clearing the cache of unnecessary information? That's what a brain dump does for your brain. Without a variety of to do's running through your mind, you can get and stay hyper-focused!

Delete and Delegate

Having done a brain dump, you are probably crazy overwhelmed right now and you hate me. I understand and won't take it personally because I want you to stick with me because I know you'll love me in a few more steps – delete and delegate.

After looking at your brain dump list, there are probably some things on there that you realize aren't that important after seeing your entire list. Maybe you wrote down a task or item that you thought you should do but no longer find important. Guess what? Just cross it off. In fact, I want you to ask yourself and truthfully answer: Does this really need to get done? Is it truly something that needs to be done now and do I really want to accomplish this?

Suddenly, you'll find more things to remove. Cross 'em off. Doesn't that feel good?

Next, of the things that really have to be done, do they have to be done by you? What can be moved off of your plate and onto someone else's? If you're a business owner with a team working with you, the choice may be obvious. If you're a solo-preneur, don't assume you can't delegate. You don't really need to do your own bookkeeping or taxes and

> *Simply, you cannot do it all nor should you attempt to. Delete and delegate to get more done.*

you can use contractors and virtual assistants for things that do not require your personal expertise. You can also delegate to your spouse, friends, neighbors, or your mom. All you have to do is ask.

Yes, it can be difficult to let others know you're overwhelmed, but if you are supposed to be the carpool driver on Thursday and are booked with client calls, ask another parent to swap with you. If the car maintenance light is on, ask your spouse if they can take it to the shop. Your kids can have age-appropriate chores that help the household continue to run smoothly.

You do not have to do everything by yourself. In fact, I highly recommend that you discontinue this mindset (and that's all it is) or you will be a slave to the clock and the stress that comes with worrying about getting it all done.

Once you've deleted and delegated, you have your true to-do list.

Do

You can now see what's left on your plate. It may still be a lot, but you'll at least have a shorter list having done your deleting and delegating. Before diving into your list, I want you to get three different colored highlighters because highlighting helps prioritization. (If you don't have highlighters, go grab three different colors of crayons from your kids. They probably have 500, so they won't miss three.)

You are going to highlight (or color) according to these categories:

1. Needs to get done right away
2. Kinda soon
3. Whenever you feel like it

It's a simple high, medium, low scale. When I have clients do this exercise, it never fails. Someone always says, "All of mine are high priority." Okay, I get that there are multiple things that are a high priority; however, I also know it's not possible for you to do them all today. So let's take that approach. Also, ask yourself what is going to move the needle on your goal? We all have the tendency to work on the little task, the easy task, the task that's more fun than the big one that is going to make the difference.

Take your "needs to get done right away" items and put them in the order in which you'll do them. You can't do 17 things at once. The beauty of this is that once they're on paper and highlighted and you know what has to be done first, second, third, etc., you'll find it far easier to focus and yes… get things done!

Create a Parking Lot

Remember your Quarterly Master 3 goals you created in the previous chapter? Well, now it's time to pick your "Daily Essential 3" goals, which will be driven by and support your Quarterly Master 3. Look at your 90-day goals and determine the best use of your time today to make those a reality. Every day, you are going to make this assessment, so you are placing the right tasks on your plate as your main focus. And yes, prioritize these three on what you should work on first, so if you happen to run out of time (there are always interruptions), you will have accomplished the most important one. So where do the rest go? That's where your parking lot comes into play.

> *Park the great ideas and goals that you have and re-visit your parking lot quarterly.*

A parking lot is the place where you park an idea or goal on which you are not currently working. When my Intentional Implementer™ clients show me their lists, they often include things that should not be their current focus. It might be something cool that they'll do in the next year or two. If you have items like that, get them off your list and into your parking lot.

For example, a client showed me her top ten to-do list. It included ten very large projects, and each one would have a massive to-do list of its own. Her tenth item was "write a book." It was clearly something that should have been in her parking lot. If you have items like this, I suggest you move them into your own parking lot. We're not saying you are not going to do it or that it's not important. Your parking lot contains those items on which you haven't started working or for which you haven't set a deadline.

Schedule It

Okay, so when I know what needs to get done, I can still be overwhelmed by my to-do list because I don't know *when* it's going to get done – when I'm going to have the time to work on it. I also know that if it is not on the calendar, it is not going to get done.

I want you to schedule your Daily Essential 3 on your calendar right now during the time you are most productive in the day. You haven't defined them yet, so simply type "Daily Essential 3" with a reasonable block of time allotted every weekday. Set it up as a recurring event. Let technology due the work rather than your brain. Your brain may forget; an automated recurring event on a calendar will not. Each day, you can specifically name your priorities and what tasks you should do to get you the results you want and enable you to reach your goals. (If you are still not using an online or automated calendar, please check out the companion course immediately at: www.implementationcode.co/freecourse)

On my calendar, you'll see 9:00 a.m. to noon blocked out for my own Daily Essential 3 that I determine every day based on my Quarterly Master 3 goals. Now if you are still working in a career for someone else, your goals may be personal and may include the things you need to do if you want to launch your own business. Your allotted time slots may be before your work day begins, at lunch, in the evenings, or on the weekend.

I also want you to schedule time to set your new 90-day Quarterly Master 3 goals and review your parking lot to determine if it's time to move something from there onto your list. I typically use the last week of each quarter (March, June, September, and December) for this and set it up as a recurring task on my calendar. I don't have to trouble my brain with remembering, and my brain appreciates that!

You may be surprised how few items actually move out of your parking lot. That's really the benefit of your parking lot – filled with things you might do but that are not overwhelming your to-do list. You'll also realize that some of your Quarterly Master 3 goals are repeats – things on which you continue to improve every 90 days. That's okay; continue improving and working toward them.

When you're getting started in picking your Quarterly Master 3, you might only pick your #1 goal to work on for the first month or two and you might not begin working on #3 until the third month. That's okay but ensure you have a plan and are itemizing daily tasks that keep moving you closer.

Now, I noted that my most productive time is in the morning. You may not think that's best for you; however, let me caution you about the law of diminishing return. You may think you're a night owl, but you will not be as productive at 10:00 p.m. as you are during the morning because of decision fatigue. It's real, and we start to feel it at the end of the day. On average, we make about 35,000 decisions per day, so saving your Daily Essential 3 until the end of your day is not in your best interest. Think you don't have the time? Make the time. Check your phone to see what your average daily screen time is. I bet there is a wealth of available time hidden there with pockets of time in places where you don't realize you're wasting it.

Stick with It

Since you are reading this book, I know you handle yourself professionally, whether you own your business or are working for someone else. So I also know that you wouldn't blow off an appointment. The goals you have scheduled are appointments with yourself, so since you wouldn't blow off anyone else, don't do it to yourself either! Show up as scheduled on your calendar and prove to yourself that these goals really do mean something. If they don't, why are they on your schedule in the first place?

> *Stop blowing yourself off. You wouldn't do it to a colleague or friend. Don't do it to YOU!*

As I write this, it's 5:30 a.m. on a Saturday. I made this appointment with myself this morning to write. Yes, it would be nice to have slept in on a Saturday, but I know that this goal is more important than that, and I show myself the importance of my goals by working on them as scheduled.

You wouldn't blow off a colleague or a friend, so stop blowing yourself off!

Finally, when you're wrapping up for the day, that is the ideal time to determine and schedule your Daily Essential 3 for the next day. That's how I handle the end of each day. By doing so, I can get right to work as soon as I show up the following day, and I'm not wasting my productive time figuring out what I should be working on. That lack of clarity quickly and easily leads to distraction.

At the end of the week on Fridays, I'm already planning out Monday and into the following week. After a few days off, it can be very difficult to figure out where you left off and how to get started again. When you schedule it on Friday, you have a clear road map on Monday morning and are immediately moving forward on your goals.

Preparation is everything!

Start Unlocking and Implementing

- Priorities shift all the time. Whatever you choose to work on reflects your priority.
- Prioritizing is the key to eliminating the sense of overwhelm.
- Your brain is better at processing information than remembering it. That's why brain dumping is critical.
- After you've brain dumped, prioritize and schedule.
- Once you delete and delegate, you have created your true to-do list.

- Everything cannot be the highest priority. Determine what tasks will move the needle toward your goals. Focus on those.
- Place the ideas and goals on which you are not currently working in your parking lot. Revisit your parking lot quarterly to determine when it's time to move them out of the lot and onto your list.
- Your list will be overwhelming until you schedule, and once scheduled, stick with it. Never blow yourself off.

Here's something to prioritize right now: Check out our companion course at:
www.implementationcode.co/freecourse

Chapter Five:

Resourcefulness: Play Full Out!

When practicing dance routines with friends back in high school, we were doing what we called "marking it," which was basically a quick run through without doing it full out. At one point, I looked in the wrong direction when I kicked and the coach called me out on it. I replied, "I'm just marking it."

The comeback: "Why would you ever mark anything incorrectly? Why would you engrain an incorrect detail in your head?"

Ouch.

Certainly, I was embarrassed that she said that in front of everyone, but she was absolutely right. If you are going to practice something incorrectly, you might as well take a seat and not do it at all. I will never forget her comment, and I think about it in all areas of my life.

If you are going to play – or even practice, for that matter – always do it full out. Give it everything and don't slack on the details. They matter.

There are five steps that I follow that allow me to play full out: establish boundaries, be resourceful, utilize every minute, find evidence of what's possible, and know your worth. Let's cover them in detail.

Establish Boundaries

Very simply: you get what you tolerate. We've already covered setting priorities, you have your color-coded calendar, have allotted the right amount of time for each activity, so you're on your road to success and nothing can stop you. Right? Wrong.

Everyone and their mother (including your own mother) is going to get in your way. They'll try to squeeze into your schedule even when there is no available time. They'll convince you to move your morning appointment, so you can join them for brunch. Notifications will blow up your phone and computer and sidetrack you. You get the picture.

In order to truly play full out and go all in, we have to set boundaries, so we can stick to what we said we are going to do and what is already reflected on our calendar. For some of you reading this, it's going to sound selfish... and it is. I am asking you to put yourself first. You and I both know that you will never be able to help anyone else if you need help yourself.

It's like the online guru who offers to teach you how to make $100k with your new business, yet she hasn't done it herself. She will never be able to help you until she's achieved it first. You need to do the work on yourself first before you start helping anyone else. Yes,

> *Never believe the motto "those who can't do, teach." Learn from someone who's done it.*

you get to be selfish in this regard, so let's walk through how to do it correctly.

First, in order to set boundaries, we have to know what a boundary is. It is simply a limit. Hopefully we all agree we need limits for everything, even things we love. Previously, we discussed creating your "ideal yes" that will be a game changer for you. But even your ideal yes requires limits. For example, responding to your mother may be an ideal yes, but talking to her six times a day is probably over your limit. You take the call because you feel obligated. She's older... what if she needs you? Thoughts start running through your head and guilt creeps in after reading her 911 text to call her. You make the call, and she invites you to Uncle Eddie's birthday party in five weeks. You tell yourself you won't respond so quickly any more; you've had enough; and then 24 minutes later, you're sucked back in.

If my mom is reading this, she knows I'm not talking about her because she knows my boundaries. She's not mad at me for having set them. She respects that I'm focused and work during the day. If she needs something, she texts before I begin my day or after I'm done saying, "Call me when you have time; no rush." Now, I have two sisters and know for a fact that she does not do this with them. Why? We've set different boundaries.

Please don't shake your head and think, "But Stacy, you don't know my mother." To that, remember the first sentence in this section: you get what you tolerate. I have some simple steps for you that enable you to train anyone to respect your boundaries.

Step 1: Advise people in advance that change is coming. Let them know you are working to be more focused and productive. If you've been addicted to email and check it and respond the second the notification pops up, people are conditioned to expect this from you. I don't suggest you make this change cold turkey. Instead, turn on an autoresponder that indicates when you will check email and how fast you'll reply. "I check emails at 11:00, 2:00, and 4:00 and will reply at that time." Now, if you've been working closely with someone, this will be a drastic change, so send them a personal heads-up about your new schedule. Give this no more than 48 hours before you put it into effect. This goes for phone calls and text messages as well. If you have frequent family callers, employees, or co-workers, let them know you are making this change to be as productive as possible and that you're placing your phone on silent until these times and that is when you'll reply or return urgent calls. For non-urgent calls, handle them at the end of the day. ***Then silence your phone and turn off notifications!*** Your business is suffering if you do not establish these boundaries.

Step 2: Stick to what you said. When someone tries to break your boundary (and I assure you, most will because they are unaccustomed to them), you must stick to your own guidelines. So if they text at 9:00 and you set your response time as 11:00, do not respond until 11:00. The second you fail to adhere to your own limits, they know the boundary doesn't really exist. After they fail to honor your boundaries for a few days or even weeks, you might wonder why. Simple. They have their own habit that they'll have to break, so you have to stick to it as long as you need to until they understand and have altered their habit. Although she doesn't do it with my sisters, my mother knows when I will and will not respond. Yes, you can train people to respect your boundaries!

Step 3: Never break your own rule. Let's say you've had a really productive day or week and are wrapping up at 12:30 but your reply timeframe is 2:00. Do not reply at 12:30, even though you have time. It's confusing, and people will quickly revert to reaching out at any time, thinking your own rules have lapsed. Lead by example. (In the free companion course, you'll learn how to draft the email at 12:30 but delay it, so the recipient thinks it was sent at 2:00. Find the link at the end of this chapter.)

In my performing arts academies, we have over 50 employees, and I only speak with one employee on a weekly basis and receive zero calls or texts from anyone other than the general manager despite about half of them having my number. I've trained them to respect my boundaries and the only texts I get from them are "happy birthday" on that day. We all actually have boundaries in place. Now that doesn't mean someone doesn't occasionally break the boundary, but it's really about what I do in those situations, not what they do. For example, a while back I received a text on a Saturday morning: "I'm sick and cannot teach today." Now we have a prescribed system in place for just such occasions, including the reporting chain… of which, in this instance, I wasn't a part. Now I could have made an exception, thinking, "He's sick, so I should step in and help." But here was my reply: "Hi, I'm so sorry to hear you aren't feeling well. Make sure to contact your manager, so she can walk you through the system we created for this situation. Feel better soon! ☺"

I'm sure there's a small percentage reading this who think I'm cold hearted, but I suspect there are many of you thinking, "Why don't I do this?!" You know exactly what happens when you say, "No problem, I'll take care of it" in any situation. They do it the next time, the time after that, and at least one more time after that. You can throw that boundary you created right out the window. Guess how many times that teacher texted me to report being sick after that first text? Zero. He learned he couldn't break my boundary.

When you don't honor your boundaries, no one else will either. When you cave and solve someone else's problem that isn't yours to solve... well, you know they are going to return again and again for the same thing. If you stick to your own systems, others will follow them as well. It's not really difficult, but it is emotionally challenging for some people. We want to be liked; we don't want to hurt feelings; we are people pleasers. Funny thing. It should work both ways but often doesn't. In the case of my sick employee, he hurt my feelings when he knew there was a reporting system but didn't follow it and tried to break my boundary. Both people play a part in this. You feel guilty that your mom calls all day, but she doesn't feel guilty knowing you're busy but calling anyway. Hello? This madness needs to stop and you know it.

One of my Intentional Implementer™ clients told me that because she works from home (and others know that), she gets countless requests for favors, especially regarding child care or picking up kids because they're stuck at work or whatever reason. She was very resentful when she unloaded on me about the situation, but all she had to do was say, "Sorry. I have to work."

> *Don't resent others' intrusions when you fail to set boundaries or don't stick to the ones you do create.*

Unfortunately, our desire to people please and have others like us and think of us as very generous leads to them suddenly taking advantage and walking all over us. Then we blame them and resent them; however, we're the ones who created the situation in the first place by either not having boundaries or not sticking to our boundaries.

Now, when you have a business and respond to customer service needs via email, phone, monitoring social media, etc., I understand your argument that you feel you need to be available 24/7 and offer a fast response time. I agree with the last part about fast response to serve clients; however, I don't think any CEO should be in the role of customer service or social media manager. Ouch. I know that hurt because a few people reading this are doing just that. Yes, when you're starting out, I know you have to wear multiple hats, but that still doesn't require immediate response. Set up autoresponders and voice mail accordingly. When business owners work with me, this is one of the first things we work on – putting automation to work and freeing up their time as quickly as possible. Hire a virtual assistant or similar on a contracted basis. Otherwise, you'll feel like your to-do list never ends and you're drowning. You whittle your inbox and voice mail down to zero… just in time for the next one to hit. You will not grow your business or get ahead when you are filling these roles.

Smart phones have allowed us to increase productivity but not without also becoming huge distractions with text message dings, email buzzes, and spam calls ringing all day. You may not realize it, but you actually have total control over your phone. Mute it or turn it over so you don't see calls coming in and turn off notifications. No one can interrupt you via your phone without you playing a role in the interruption. I've been good at setting boundaries and was able to keep my phone on, but then the telemarketer calls starting hitting… several times a day. I found myself getting very annoyed and wanted to answer just to tell them to stop calling when I realized I am in control. I silenced my phone. It's so easy to blame others, but you are always in control of setting and maintaining your boundaries.

Be Resourceful

In order to succeed, you don't have to be smart or excellent or even good. You have to be willing to learn. Your openness to education is what will take you far. Playing full out means being resourceful. It doesn't matter what resources you have… or don't have. It matters how resourceful you are, and there's a difference.

One of my four company values is resourcefulness. My team knows that I don't expect them to *know* all the answers, but I expect them to *find* the answers. The answer to almost everything is online and can be uncovered with a search engine that delivers literally countless articles and videos on every topic. If you get stuck using certain software, you'll find the developer's support and tech help online… and you'll find plenty of other users who have the solution you need as well. If something isn't working with our email, my team knows to reach out to the provider for the solution rather than telling me it doesn't work or that they can't figure it out. I hold myself to those standards as well.

Never stop looking for the answer. There is always a way. Too many people stop too soon and give up. The thing you are trying to get to work won't work until you find the solution. It's like the earlier analogy of the person whose car is stuck in the mud. Keep searching and trying different things and tweaking what you are doing until you've gotten it right.

My husband and I own rental properties. Our first short-term rental was a lake house with a hot tub – a feature that made it very attractive. The hot tub broke in early May, so I called around for a repair service and was told it would be four to six weeks until he could get there… "It's hot tub season and everyone wants theirs running. We're booked solid." That wasn't going to work. We already had rental reservations, and I knew we'd have to offer refunds or discounts without a working hot tub. There was a likelihood of getting bad reviews as well that would impact future bookings. There was a lot at stake financially. I pleaded my case to him, but "no, sorry" continued to be the reply.

I stopped to consider the facts. I'd already called several companies and he was the only one who'd even taken my call in the first place. He said there was no way to squeeze me in. Some people might throw up their hands and simply wait the four to six weeks. I decided to sleep on it and continue to dig for a creative solution. Knowing I didn't have the four to six weeks to wait nor did I want to incur financial loss on the bookings, I phoned him back in the morning and asked if perhaps he had someone on staff who'd be willing to work overtime and I'd pay the premium. He said he could handle it that way in two days. Bingo. Yes, I was willing to pay more for the service, but even paying for overtime, we'd come out ahead financially.

> *The more you want it, the more resourceful you become.*

This isn't a huge example of resourcefulness. Yes, I had to make a lot of phone calls, but I only had to come up with one more idea for a solution – the overtime approach.

Sometimes we have to keep going and thinking and trying and starting over repeatedly until we get the answer we need and want. And you will... when you want it badly enough.

As I was working on this chapter, the coronavirus pandemic hit, and as I write this, my performing arts academies are completely shut down with no set date to reopen. Talk about having to be resourceful! I'd been preparing for a recession with a reduction in revenue and our numbers, but never in a million years thought about this situation unfolding as it has. During the last recession, we managed okay because parents wanted to keep their kids in classes as long as they could to maintain some normalcy. This time, that same caring parent wants their kids safe and at home as soon as possible. While I didn't prepare for this scenario, this is where the scrappy, resourceful entrepreneurs survive while those who fail to look for new and different opportunities crumble. The first week of the closure, my team and I came up with virtual lessons. We thought it was the obvious choice, but we were the only studio to offer it in our area. The others simply closed. I'm sure there are refund requests coming in daily, but we only have had six students out of over 900 quit outright. How? Why? We're resourceful. No does not mean no. It just means find another way. We're hashing out plans for every other possible scenario now. Recessions are cyclical, which is why I was actually preparing for the next one when the pandemic hit. I was in business in 2008 and went through the "great recession," so I wanted us to be as prepared as possible. Yes, the current situation far exceeds my expectation, but we continue to be resourceful.

Now, let me explain: There is a difference between quitting and knowing when it's time to walk away from a goal. Sometimes I set goals only to realize in their pursuit that they are no longer important to me. The situation or circumstances may have changed. I'm not quitting because it's difficult; I'm walking away because its priority has changed or evaporated completely.

Check in when you are thinking of letting go to really be sure you understand the reason. When I take on things I really don't want to do (i.e., I've failed to prioritize correctly from the start), I end up procrastinating. Procrastination is a sure indicator of a lack of importance to me. My advice to you: Don't try to do things you don't really want to do or you won't be as resourceful as you need to be and you won't play full out. True success stories find a way to their happy endings when most others give up.

Utilize Every Minute

The biggest complaint I hear from clients is, "I don't have enough time." We all have the same 24 hours each and every day. So how do some people get twice as much done in a day? I've had the privilege of conducting calendar audits for my Intentional Implementer™ clients, so I see exactly where some people use their time wisely and others waste it. Admittedly, it's easier to see other's flaws so much clearer than your own. That said, I've personally gotten much more efficient by seeing other people's time wasters.

When we covered the concept of starting small, I cautioned you against "all or nothing" type thinking. The same thing applies when it comes to using your time wisely. That "all or nothing" attitude will kill your efficiency and automatically set you up to waste time. Let's say you do 30-minute daily workouts and you slept in on Saturday. The rest of your day is packed, and now you only have about 15 minutes to work out. Do you do it or not? Most people skip it. But working out for 15 minutes is 15 times better than a zero-minute workout.

The same thing applies on your work calendar. Let's say someone cancels a 30-minute appointment at the last minute, and you have a very large project to work on. You may decide not to apply those 30 minutes because the project will take far longer, so will that time really make a difference? The answer: yes. Don't waste a single minute. Now you may think your time will be better spent answering emails, but that task may break the boundary you've set for that. Be careful! When you have time set aside for a project and you end early, it is not the time to mindlessly scroll through your phone. Be productive!

For those who claim they don't have time, take a look at your daily routine. I am certain you will *find* time. For example, I work out in my home gym – nothing fancy, a few weights, a mat, and a bench. Do I do that to save money? No. In fact, I have a gym membership and also pay for virtual classes. I do it to save time when needed. My commute to and from my home gym is 30 seconds. When I can't get to the gym, I can still work out for at least a few minutes. I'm always dialed in to shaving time whenever possible. When I take my kids to gymnastics, I take my computer or a book; after I drop them off at school, I listen to a podcast on the way home; while I get ready in the morning, I watch virtual coaching classes for a program I pay for. You get the picture. I'm sure you can also shave minutes and find time.

Don't get me wrong. I am not suggesting you work constantly. You must take a break to refresh and refuel. I end my work day at 3:00 p.m., so I can pick the kids up after school, and I do not go back to work in the evenings. I also don't work on Saturdays and Sundays. Utilizing every minute isn't about working 24/7. It's about getting the most out of your time.

Find Evidence

Find evidence of what's possible and also what goes on behind the scenes. It's hard to play full out unless you know what "full out" looks like. For example, you may spend an hour a week on marketing only to find out that I spend three hours a day on it. Without knowing what's possible, you also don't know what's optimal.

To really know what's possible, optimal, and what goes on behind the scenes, surround yourself with people who are already doing it. I never thought I could write a book, but I found myself in the company of people who've written best sellers. Suddenly, I realized it was

> *"Don't get creative. Model what works."*
>
> *~ Tony Robbins*

possible and learned what was needed and had the support of people who'd already accomplished what I wanted to do.

Understand what the evidence really is, and that means really looking behind the scenes. In dance, there is the on-stage performance and then there is practice. Many people only see what happens on the stage. They don't see the blood, sweat, and tears that go into delivering a beautifully executed performance. That's why you have to look behind the scenes to fully understand what it takes.

If you want to look like a Victoria Secret model, you have to see what she eats, how and when she works out, what kinds of workouts she does, etc. Knowing that can be intimidating, but you have to get a clear picture of what it takes to achieve what you want – what's normal and what's optimal.

If you only see the end result, you're not getting the right picture. Maybe you see the amazing success of other entrepreneurs, but you aren't getting the same results, so you start to feel defeated. I assure you, every entrepreneur has plenty of flops. I once spent $3,000 on a contractor who completely disappeared the next day – with my money – and never spoke to me again. Everyone who's ever achieved success has plenty of failures, false starts, and missteps, so don't feel defeated when things don't go as smoothly as it seems to for others. It's all part of entrepreneurship. Keep that in mind when the going gets tough. Get back up and start taking action again.

Show up, play full out, be consistent.

Know Your Worth

You absolutely have to know what you're worth and exactly what you bring to your business. Why? Without this knowledge, you won't know what to put on your plate and what to delegate.

There are plenty of entrepreneurs who fail to know what they're worth. They end up spending their days on $10/hour tasks and then wonder why they're only making $20,000. I can tell them why: it's the math. If you spend 40 hours a week on $10/hour tasks, you'll bring in $400, and doing that for 52 weeks a year becomes $20,800... $20,000 if you want to give yourself two weeks off. In order to make more at that rate, you have to work more hours. But even working 60 hours only adds another $10,000 annually, and I'm sure you don't want to work that many hours. You're worth so much more.

You have to know exactly what you're worth, so you can start building your dream team. Don't spend your time on administrative tasks in your business because you'll be working for a far lower hourly rate than you are worth. Hire or contract an assistant. Spend your time in your area of expertise, whatever that may be, so you are earning the hourly rate you deserve. I'm sure it's far higher than $10 or $20.

Even if you don't have your own business yet but are working toward building one, you should still have a dream team to help. If you are still working for someone else while you are working to launch your business, you know how little time you may have. Should you really be spending that time on household chores, cleaning, laundry, or landscaping? Rather than spending all day Saturday on those tasks, you should be recharging. By building a team, you've actually purchased the time you need to be in your zone of genius or to rest and refuel to be at your best. This is also true for any entrepreneur who's already launched their business. Their zone of genius is worth 100 times what they pay to delegate other tasks.

No matter your situation, if you don't have an assistant, you *are* the assistant. If you think you can't afford one and your personal hourly worth is $100, you're actually paying $100/hour for an assistant. You're too expensive to spend your time that way. You'd never pay $100/hour for an assistant, and when you look at it from that perspective, $10 or $15/hour for a virtual assistant or similar is suddenly very affordable.

In my Foot Traffic Formula coaching program, one of the first things I teach small business owner is how to hire, train, and maximize their social media managers, so they can get the most out of their businesses and live and enjoy the lives they want and dream about. Building your dream team is a necessity for you to truly play full out... and do so without burning out.

Start Unlocking and Implementing

- If you fail to set boundaries, you'll always get what you tolerate.
- Steps to training others to respect your boundaries:
  - Advise people of a change, and silence your phone and turn off notifications.
  - Stick to what you've set.
  - Never break your own rule.
- You don't need to be excellent to succeed, but you do have to be willing to learn.
- Use every minute wisely. It's not about working constantly; it's about getting the most out of your time.
- When you really look at your daily routine, you'll find places where you can carve out more time.

- To really know what's possible, optimal, and what goes on behind the scenes, surround yourself with people who are already doing it.
- Unless you know your true worth, you'll end up spending time on $10/hour tasks when you could be earning $100/hour instead.

Want to really play full out? Check out our companion course at:

www.implementationcode.co/freecourse

Chapter Six

Accountability: Answer to Someone

We all have that certain someone in our life who's a big talker. You know the one. The one who always *says* they're going to do something, but you know that it's all talk – the friend who always says she's going to lose weight and is starting a new diet every month, the neighbor who's always talking about launching his own business yet you see him leave for his corporate job every day like clockwork, your relative who's always talking about getting out of debt but just bought a new boat with no money down. The list goes on.

I know you pictured one or two people guilty of talking big without delivering on what they say, and you and I both know that we can sometimes be that very person as well. Accountability is one of the toughest aspects of entrepreneurship. Being your own boss means there's no one to really hold you accountable. Moreover, if you've launched your business without any managerial experience in your former career, you may have no idea about how to hold your team accountable. You may think it's your team's fault when results aren't happening, but if you're honest, deep down, you know you have to develop better leadership skills.

Accountability is a critical component to the success of... well, everything. That's the very reason we include accountability coaching in our Foot Traffic Formula program. We want our clients to get results, and we know they won't unless someone is holding them accountable. In fact, in the program, we ask why people join, and nine times out of ten, the reason they mention is the need for accountability.

As cited in numerous online articles, a study by the American Society of Training and Development revealed that there's a 65 percent chance of accomplishing a goal if you commit to someone. If you really want your chances to soar, create an accountability appointment with the person to whom you've committed. Chance of success then goes up to 95 percent. So yes, accountability is a linchpin to success.

> *Accountability is the glue that bonds commitment to results.*

Did you notice the important aspect of that study? There's another person involved. It's a very rare successful entrepreneur who gets results simply by self-discipline; however, there are ways to ensure you are holding yourself accountable.

More than Self-Discipline

First, understand and be very clear about what you want to do and what you are signing up for. Before you set a goal, know why you want to achieve it and educate yourself on the steps you'll need to take. Yes, this probably sounds familiar by now, but knowing your why is foundational to achieving anything.

Recently, I wanted to learn more about silver and gold investing. Simply assuming it was the right strategy for me would be a mistake, so I needed to know everything about it. I read a ton of books, found a knowledgeable investment guru on YouTube, talked with a few friends who were involved in this type of investing, and talked to my own CPA about the pros and cons. There was no shortage of self-education. I needed to know everything before deciding if I wanted to commit to this.

If you commit too early and without all the facts (or at least without dedicating yourself to learning as much as you possibly can), you'll find yourself in trouble. You may start pursing a goal that is not at all right for you. Yes, there's a difference between quitting outright and deciding that the path you started on isn't right for you. By educating yourself from the outset, you can avoid heading down the wrong path, wasting time and perhaps money as well.

Next, remind yourself. And remind yourself repeatedly. As you'll recall, when I had you create your Quarterly Master 3 goals, I told you to post them so that you see them regularly. Maybe it's a Post-it® note on your monitor, bathroom mirror, refrigerator… or all three places. The more you see that note, the more it serves as an accountability reminder. Maintain your hyper-focus on your goals.

Schedule it. Your calendar is a great tool for self-accountability. Do your brain dump, prioritize, and start assigning time on your calendar. Decide your starting point and take an educated guess on how long it will take to achieve your goal, and then break that down into daily or weekly allotments. Maybe you allot five hours every Friday to your project, or maybe it's so important that it needs to consume five hours every day. Depending on your schedule, you may need to use weekend time, so schedule two hours every Saturday and block that on your calendar until it's done.

If it's not on your calendar, it will always take much longer than expected and runs the risk of not being finished at all. Again, if you find yourself not making time for it, it's time to circle back and ask yourself how much you really want this. While I'm a big believer in education, I'll caution you to ensure you're making time to "do" and not just learn. Entrepreneurs have a tendency to consume more than we create. This is where you'll need to apply the 80/20 rule – consume (or learn) only 20 percent of the time and spend the other 80 percent doing and creating. If you are working that ratio in reverse, I know for a fact that you are wasting way too much time.

Finally, once you are ready to commit to a goal, tell people... even shout it out loud! Get over your fear of failing and worrying about what may happen if you don't achieve what you set out to do. I'm sometimes still nervous to tell my team about my goals, but the more I share, the more they encourage me to go even bigger. Yes, goals can be private, and if you really feel that going public is too paralyzing, then keep them private... but I have to ask: If you aren't ready to tell others, are you really committed to this goal?

Too often, we fear what others may say or think, but I assure you, when the right people hear my goals, it helps immensely. People aren't mind readers, and we have no idea what is going on in each other's heads. For example, if you set a goal to get out of debt and share that, a good friend may stop you if you suggest going out for dinner and offer a less expensive alternative. They may even call you out on it: "I thought you said you were sticking to a budget?" Friends can help you stay on track and keep moving to achieve your goals… well, the *right* friends can.

Birds of a Feather

Birds of a feather flock together. If you've heard that but aren't sure its meaning, it means that people with the same interests and tastes will be found together. Let me share an equally important phrase: Show me your friends and I'll show you your results. So true!

> *"You are the average of the five people you spend the most time with."*
>
> *~ Jim Rohn*

It is time to uplevel your inner circle. If your friends aren't achieving or even interested in achieving the same things that you want, it's time to find new friends.

I enjoy assessing the five people with whom I spend the most time several times a year. I do it regularly because it changes. I write down who those five people are and honestly consider the impact they're having. It could be your spouse, parent, best friend, colleague or co-worker, or maybe a favorite podcast. Yes, I absolutely consider the latter as one of my five because it reflects where I'm spending my time and what the podcaster is saying and putting into my brain. It is someone who I'm surrounding myself with despite the fact that we've never met in person. I spend more time listening to the podcaster than my mom.

Stop right now and take time to write down the five people with whom you spend the most time. Once you've noted them, do some comparisons:

- How much money do I make compared to them?
- How healthy am I compared to them?
- How driven am I compared to them?
- How well do I uphold my values compared to them?
- How _____ (you fill in the blank) am I compared to them?

Keep in mind that your comparison is the average, and if you are the average of your five people, you'll quickly see how this exercise can help you achieve more and uplevel your game.

I know that someone who picks up this book and is still around in Chapter 6 does not consider themselves or refer to themselves as average, so I know it's not a word that you associate with yourself either. If, through the comparison exercise you just did, you think you're at the top because you're the wealthiest, smartest, and fittest in your group, you may think you've won. Well, I have bad news. The most dangerous place to be is at the top. You are being held back if you're there right now. There isn't much, if any, room for growth, and you have no evidence about what more is possible... what more you can create. It's a lot of weight to carry around, knowing you have to be the innovator of everything without role models to emulate.

Some of us certainly like being at the top, the star student, athlete, or musician. We like to be recognized for being the best – the smartest, strongest, fittest, richest, and so on. However, you have to accept not being *the* best in order to become *your* best... even if that means being at the bottom or well below average of your top five people. Honestly, as I write this, I find myself at the bottom of my top five. And that's good. The knowledge, inspiration, and big ideas that come from the people who are smarter, faster, and more experienced than I am is incredible. I'm working my way up to being in the middle of my group! One day, I may wake up and discover that I've transitioned to the top, and that's when it will be time to switch it up... and change the "birds" with whom I hang out.

Let's say you realize you are in the middle rank of your group or even near or at the top. It's time to fix that ASAP! First, identify who you'd like to see in your top five, and then start playing your part to reach out, connect, and show them some love. Don't just ask. Think about how you could give value and serve them. You don't get into a new circle by being the needy person, so don't show up with a list of things you want their help with. You need to offer some value as well. I've been invited into circles not by the result I had at the time but because I'm resourceful and work on self-education, so I had some of the latest strategies to share with the group.

> *It feels good to be at the top, but when you're there, there's not much room for growth.*

Don't throw yourself a pity party that you can't uplevel yet because you aren't good enough. Continue to work on yourself. This process is like climbing a staircase... not taking an elevator to the top. No one can stop you from picking a mentor and following them from afar. Maybe you can't connect with someone making ten times as much as you. You can't take them to lunch every day, but you can listen to them at lunch every day. It still positively impacts you.

Partner Up

Take your top five people one step further and partner up. Have one of your top five be your official coach, mastermind colleague, or accountability buddy. But give this decision a good deal of thought because your selection could be a make-or-break decision. Consider the degree to which this person will advance your top five and how it affects your overall average.

If you think you got a steal of a deal on a mastermind and wonder why others are charging so much, ask yourself about the level of the group's participants. Are they really going to help you uplevel and grow? You might think that saving money with your choice is a financial advantage; however, your decision may end up costing you a lot more in the long run. I'm not saying that the quality of the mastermind is always directly proportional to the amount that you spend, but if we're being honest, we typically get what we pay for. Sometimes saving money can cost us a lot more than we realize.

Now, I understand that you may not currently be in a position to make this investment… although I truly believe that it's always the right time to invest in your own growth. Regardless, you can still find an accountability partner for free, but in the same way that I cautioned you about selecting a paid group, I'll caution you about your partner choice. You have to pick the right person. Pick a person who you know will hold you accountable, who will give you honest feedback and tough love… not just someone who will tell you what you want to hear and let you off the hook time and again. Will this person really push you? At the same time, you'll be providing honest, tough love feedback to them.

When you select someone who is equally motivated, the two of you can be off to the races, pushing and encouraging each other to get things done. Set aside time to talk frequently, at least once a week, to discuss each other's goals and talk about progress. And never lie about your progress. Your accountability partner may be impressed, but you're only hurting yourself. Go into the relationship with the understanding that at some point one of you may really take off, so it will be time to change partners.

You want to ensure that your partner – at all times – is setting big goals and taking action. If you have someone who continually blows off your meetings or fails to meet their goals, you'll almost always start to make excuses for yourself too. Birds of a feather and all that. Go getters only for your accountability partner! If your partner is someone who pushes you and that you admire, you'll stick with them and be accountable to them and to yourself. Another great option is to join groups of like-minded people. If you're a small business owner, I want to invite you to join my free Facebook group at www.FootTrafficCommunity.com.

Accountability Insights

Once you find the right mastermind group or accountability partner, here are a few things to remember:

- Your word is important. When you go against your word, you lose people's faith and trust in you and what you say.

- When you say things out loud, they come back to you. For example, on one of my podcasts, I shared that we'd be hiring additional accountability coaches and sales reps in the next few months, and I immediately had someone reach out who wanted to be a coach. It wasn't someone I would have thought of, but by saying it out loud and raising awareness, she talked to us, and it clicked.

- Speak up to get what you want. When we purchased a home as an investment property, we had to furnish the entire thing, and that's a huge undertaking and very expensive. So we started telling people about it, and the more we shared, the more people gave. We got free bedroom sets, kitchen table, pool table, and so much more. Many people told us if we'd haul it away, it was ours for free. Speak up!

- Remember that you are surrounding yourself with the right people – people who are able to help you with your goals, whether that is just giving encouragement, making a connection for you, or being able to help you actually get it done.

- The more you talk about it, the more you think about it. It keeps it top of mind – like that Post-it® note that is always in your line of sight.

- Don't keep secrets. Keeping it a secret does nothing to help you prioritize. The more people you have asking, "How's it going?" the more accountability you have to get it done.

Rewards are important. Your brain loves working toward pleasure, so reward yourself. Set a reward for specific tasks completed toward your goal. For example, when I have 21 check marks toward one of my goals, my spouse and I go out to that nice restaurant we've wanted to visit. Or every time I complete that daily to-do, I take a 15-20 minute break to go outside and clear my head. When I complete this to-do list weekly for a month, I schedule a massage. You get the idea.

Ensure that your reward system is not hurting your ultimate goal. If your goal is to get out of debt, your reward for saving all week cannot be to hit the mall for a shopping excursion on Saturday. If you want to lose weight, your reward for eating healthy Monday through Friday can't be to overindulge on the weekend. Instead, if you don't spend money all week, treat yourself and your family to a hike and picnic in the park. If you stick to your healthy eating regime, get your nails done.

When you want to unlock the secret to getting it all done, accountability is the key you need!

Start Unlocking and Implementing

- Being your own boss means there's no one else to hold you accountable, and it is tough to do it yourself.
- When you are accountable to someone else, studies show a marked increase in the chance of success.
- Commit to what you want to do, remind yourself repeatedly, and be sure you schedule it on your calendar.
- You can't just learn. You have to do too. Spend only 20 percent of your time learning and 80 percent of your time doing.
- Remember that you are the average of the five people with whom you spend the most time. Being at the top of the group leaves no real room for growth.
- Accept not being *the* best in order to become *your* best.
- Find the right mastermind group and/or accountability partner. Use tough love and honest feedback to hold each other to what you've agreed to do.
- Speak up. When you say things aloud, they have a way of coming back to you.
- Reward yourself appropriately.

Improve your accountability. Check out our companion course at:
www.implementationcode.co/freecourse

Chapter Seven:

Implementation Action Plan

Congratulations! You actually made it to the last chapter. However, you probably have your own individual thought about getting to this point right now. Stop and ask yourself: What are you thinking? How do you feel? Do you feel empowered, confident, ready to move forward? If not, don't worry. I've worked with enough high performers to know that the thought in your head right now may very well be: "I still don't know where to start."

Let's stop that thought and get to work because now it's time to start implementing your action plan.

You can do anything you want... *anything*. But you can't do *everything*. At least not at once. It's time we pick our favorites, and we put everything else on pause.

How many times have you heard that you shouldn't have favorites? Having favorites is not fair. As someone who owns two children's performing arts academies, I have been accused of having favorite dancers. When I stopped teaching dance and started teaching small business owners, I even heard the same thing from adults – that I have favorites who are featured on my podcasts or invited to speak on stage at my events.

You may expect me to deny that and tell you I don't have favorites, but here's the thing: I actually do. I will tell parents and clients to their faces that I 100 percent have favorites. You may be thinking that it isn't fair and that everyone should have a chance. That's just it – I do give everyone a chance. Every single person who comes in contact with me has a chance to be one of my favorites. My favorites are people who show up, are consistent, do the work, try new things, experiment, fail, and get back up again.

You can probably figure out my least favorites. They're the ones who expect to get everything without lifting a finger, who complain that they should be making more money by now, who contend that this doesn't work for them like everyone else, and who come up with a million other excuses why things aren't working. Are you shocked by that? Are you shocked by the descriptions of my favorites and least favorites? No, of course not.

> *Guess what? It is really okay to have favorites. It's also okay to fully embrace them.*

Now if you've held onto the belief that you shouldn't have favorites and that concept is so tightly engrained in your mind, it is time to let it go.

If someone has told you that you needed to balance yourself out, working on your weaknesses and not just your strengths, I couldn't disagree more! It's time to lean into your favorites, to find your strengths, and double down. You with me? It's time to pick your own favorites.

Your Mastery

No one wants to hire someone who's an expert at everything. An expert at everything probably doesn't exist.

Imagine there's a crack in your home's foundation. It is really bad and needs to be repaired correctly. You find two companies to check it out and provide a quote. The first business is Bob's Home Fixin' Services. Bob is an all-around handyman and can fix "pretty much anything." You ask if he's ever done this sort of repair before and he tells you he has. The second company to stop by is Home Foundation Services. Foundation repairs are what they do all day and every day. It is the only thing they do, and they're experts. They tell you that the crack in your foundation isn't even the worst one they've seen and repaired.

If the estimates you receive are similarly priced, which one do you choose? No doubt, the experts. If the price from Home Foundation Services is double that of Bob's Home Fixin' Services, which one do you choose now? Most people will still opt for the expert because they know if it isn't done right, they'll have to pay to repair it again or face an even bigger, more expensive problem. They won't be calling Bob for this job.

Everyone has something they were born to do. Everyone is an expert at something. Your expertise is almost always one of your "favorites." It's possible you haven't discovered it yet, but that's okay. Keep taking massive action, and you will get there faster. When you find your expertise, double down.

Your Focus & Goals

Once you are clear on the end result, it is time to pick and choose your goals and focus wisely. No more doing things simply because they are on your to-do list. Remember: We aren't trying to be busy; we are trying to be productive… producing results.

When you focus your goals on revenue-generating activities, you will take your business (or someone else's) where you (or your employer) want it to go. Even if you are an employee, contractor, or freelancer working for someone else, if you focus on revenue-generating activities as your number one goal for the company you work for, that business owner is not going to complain or be angry. Just the opposite!

This needs to go hand in hand with what actually gets scheduled on your calendar. When you find your top, most effective revenue-generating activities, those need to show up on your calendar. Your goals and focus must work together. If you have goals but don't focus on them... well, you might as well not even bother writing them down. They are doing you no good.

> *Revenue-generating activities should always have a top spot on your to-do list.*

Recharging Activities

Yes, you should have something called free time. It should occur every day and on the weekends. You need to recharge. People used to ask me, "What do you do for fun? What hobbies do you have?" Early on, as an adult, I honestly couldn't answer. I liked work. But... when I realized that I produced my best work after a break from it and a recharge, I was all in.

When I recharge, I like to go for a walk or bike ride, and I enjoy swimming with the kids in the summer. For self-care, I put on face masks, take a warm bath, and listen to soothing spa music. I'm practically obsessed with massages. I love traveling, and tropical beaches are a favorite destination... and when I go, I leave my computer behind in Milwaukee. I also like to have family movie night on Fridays and don't jam pack the weekend with a million things. My perfect weekend is wide open for family time, when my computer stays in my office and I don't go in there.

This is a hard one for many of my Intentional Implementer™ clients. They've been so busy working in their careers that recharging hasn't been on their to-do list or scheduled on their calendar, so it hasn't happened. Take some time to figure out what recharging looks like for you and what is your favorite thing to do. Yes, you are allowed to have favorites!

Don't overlook alone time. It's important. I love my family, but being alone is also necessary. If you have kids and are married, take turns. My husband and I switch taking the kids to school, helping with homework, putting them to bed, and all the other things that are required. One does the task while the other takes a break for some alone time. We used to do everything together, but we realized taking turns presented the golden opportunity for each of us to have some time to recharge. When I take the kids to gymnastics, my husband goes to the gym for his own workout. The following week, we swap. If you happen to be a single parent, we'll talk more about getting help shortly.

Letting Go

It is time to see less of certain people, and you know exactly who I'm talking about, don't you? Be okay with letting go of some of these relationships. It's time to say goodbye to certain ones. Now, before you call your BFF from high school that you still hang out with and let her know you're moving on to bigger and better things, please don't. You don't have to make any sort of announcement. Simply focus on where you want your energy to go. When you stop calling as often and do not reply as quickly, these relationships will naturally fade.

Maybe you have a certain friend but know that this person is not someone who will help you level up. Do you have to let the relationship go? No, of course not. As you'll recall, you are the average of the five people with whom you spend the most time, so just make sure this person isn't in your top five. There are friends and people you talk to weekly, monthly, every six months, or once a year.

> *Evaluate relationships, tasks, and goals and decide if it may be time to let them go.*

That's completely fine. You have to decide what kind of relationship it will be for you.

There are some tasks you do because you've always done them or everyone says you have to be doing them, so you feel obligated to do it too. I am here to tell you that you get to be the boss of what you do (unless, of course, you have a real boss, but stick with me and we'll change that real quick).

When I say let go, it isn't just about relationships or tasks. It may also be time to let go of some goals you've been holding onto for a long time. They may even be goals that someone else set for you or expects of you. Maybe your mom thinks you need to have someone significant in your life, but it's not important to you. Let it go.

Free Education

I am a huge fan of podcasts, and I listen to them several days each week. It is such a great way to consume content, and the best part is that they're free. In fact, I started my podcast, "Foot Traffic," in 2017 and still record new content weekly because I know how powerful podcasts are for the consumer. I want small business owners who are busy and feeling overwhelmed to stay productive.

Personally, I think podcasts are so much more productive than social media. For example, when you listen to a podcast, are you interrupted or distracted by someone else's podcast, becoming the victim of shiny object syndrome? Not usually. You typically listen to the podcasts you like from beginning to end. Now, how often do you consume content on social media without becoming distracted by something else on the feed? Social media can take you down a rabbit hole. Now I'm not saying I don't consume content on social media; however, I prefer podcasts because it keeps me focused.

Don't listen to 72 different podcasts. Pick a few mentors who don't contradict each other or you'll be going in circles. Currently, I have two mentors whose podcasts I listen to. I consume every word (and it's a lot of content), but I get to go deeper into the information rather than reading bits and pieces and suffering from shiny object syndrome. They complement one another, and it keeps me on my path. If you listen to too many, you are bound to hear contradictory information. You'll start working on a plan and then scrap it when another podcaster or mentor suggests something different.

I've created "The Implementation Code" podcast to go along with what I've covered in this book. That would be a great place for you to start!

Your Coach

You get what you pay for. If you stay in the world of free, you are missing out. Most mentors (and podcasters) who put time and energy into free content offer something even better in their paid programs. Honestly, I've had a business coach since I was 21. When people ask how I've accomplished so much already, the answer is simple: a coach. I hired someone who had already done what I wanted to achieve. They taught me how to do it faster than if I were to figure it out on my own. I value time; I value speed. That is how I get so much done in so little time.

> **Without fail, you always get what you pay for.**

A coach can tell you, "Don't do that. I tried it and it didn't work." They'll tell you what to say to a client and share their own experiences. They've been there and done that.

Make sure you aren't getting a bargain coach! Don't brag about how you got a steal of a deal. Do you think the NBA is hiring bargain coaches... or getting the best of the best instead? If you are on a tight budget, rather than shopping for a bargain, you might be better off learning from the coach you can't afford for free (via podcasts, groups, etc.). Then save every penny until you are ready to make the hire. If I could go back in time and get my money back from all the "bargain" courses, coaches, and masterminds, I could take that money and hire any coach in the world.

Do your due diligence and check out who you are hiring. When I became a business coach, people were shocked to learned that I had an actual business before I started my coaching business. It's surprising how many business coaches are out there who have never owned a business besides their coaching/consulting firm. It's scary. If they don't have real experience, where are they getting this knowledge and information from? Find someone who actually has the experience. It will save you so much time and money!

Dealing with Least Favorites

While I want you to double down on your favorites, I also know that there will always be your least favorite things that still have to be done.

First, and perhaps most important, decide if anything on your least favorite list really needs to happen. If not, say goodbye and move on.

If least favorites do need to happen and you don't want to (or can't) do them yourself, you have three options.

Pay someone else to do it. There is someone else out there who loves to do the thing you hate or suck at. Hate laundry? Someone will gladly do it and has built their own business around other people's laundry. Don't have time to cook? There are meal services and meal prep companies that will deliver right to your door. Feel like you are always cleaning? Someone near you has already started this small business because they have a passion for it. You don't have to do the things you don't want to do. This also goes for business tasks. Hate math? Hire a bookkeeper or tax accountant. Stay focused on your mastery and hire out the rest, so you can stay in your zone of genius.

Ask for help. Help doesn't always have to cost money. Ask a friend to swap babysitting services with you.

You'll take her kids, so she can enjoy date night, and then the next week, you swap.

Know your resources. You are busy and don't have to (nor can you) do it all. For example, I had a number of speaking engagements coming up, and I needed to get several new outfits, but I kept dreading spending time to get this done. So I texted my free stylist at Nordstrom (yes, you can have one too) and told her that I needed to come in and get a few outfits. I sent her a digital board of outfit ideas I liked within my budget. A few days later, I walked into the store and headed right to the fitting room. She was there with a rack full of things I would have picked out in my size, and she kept checking on me. It's free. I've done this dozens of times. They're not pushy or salesy, just helpful. Free. When I told a friend about it, she said she'd feel guilty taking advantage of this service. They actually *want* you to take advantage... that's why they created it. And to be completely transparent, they made a ton of money off me that day.

Know your resources and take full advantage of them. They are a win/win for everyone involved.

Here are the final thoughts I want to leave with you. No matter what you do from here on out, just don't stop implementing. Keep taking massive action. It's the best thing you can do. I also want you to show up for *yourself* and bring your best. If you work from home, it can be tempting to stay in your PJs or yoga pants with a messy bun. Don't. Save that for the weekend when you're recharging. I want you to show up showered and dressed for the day.

Here's why. Not only have I coached thousands of small business owners, I've coached thousands of dancers.

Some of them showed up in pajama pants, but the dancers who showed up in their leotard and tights showed up differently and performed better. When I started to see this difference, we implemented a dress code and required dance attire. You must think, feel, and show up as the person you want to be. You don't magically change once you do. You change now and start to see results later.

We didn't get to talk about certain habits, like what high performers eat, drink, and how they take care of their bodies. And that is just scratching the surface of more that I could have covered in this book. But don't worry. I've added all that and more in the free companion course that goes with *The Implementation Code*. Your immediate to-do? Download your free resources and your implementation checklist on what to do next now that you've finished the book. This is your next best step.

Go grab it now at www.implementationcode.co/freecourse.

I'll look for you there!

Start Unlocking and Implementing

- It is definitely okay to have favorites. Figure out what yours are.
- Focus on your mastery. People want to hire experts rather than jack-of-all-trade types.
- When revenue-producing activities are at the top of your list, everyone wins.
- Take time to recharge. No matter how much you love your work, you'll be so much better at it when you take time away.

- Let go of the relationships, tasks, and goals that aren't serving you.
- Podcasts are a great way to educate yourself and offer fewer distractions than social media.
- Hire a coach, but do your due diligence in finding one.
- When something must be done and you don't like it or have the skills, figure out another way to get it done.

Chapter Eight

Case Studies

Finally, I'd like to share some of the comments and photos I've received from a few of my Intentional Implementer™ clients to give you a real-world sense of what my Intentional Implementer™ Mastery Program can do for you as well!

Candace Starr

"I am new to Foot Traffic Formula as of this year. I have been watching Stacy from afar for about two years... yes, two years. Being a dance studio owner, I felt really connected to her and all she represented in the online space. I literally was a newbie on the block years ago with zero knowledge of online lingo. But it was a time leap and here I am.

"I said all that because the moment I joined Foot Traffic Formula, Stacy presented her week one Intentional Implementer™ Mastery Program video and I was hooked. Simplistic as it was to **clean up my office and organize it**, Stacy's style was a game changer.

"Then it was the **calendar creation**... another game changer. On to **triggers** and **boundaries**.

"I'm thankful for Stacy, her team, and all her amazing systems."

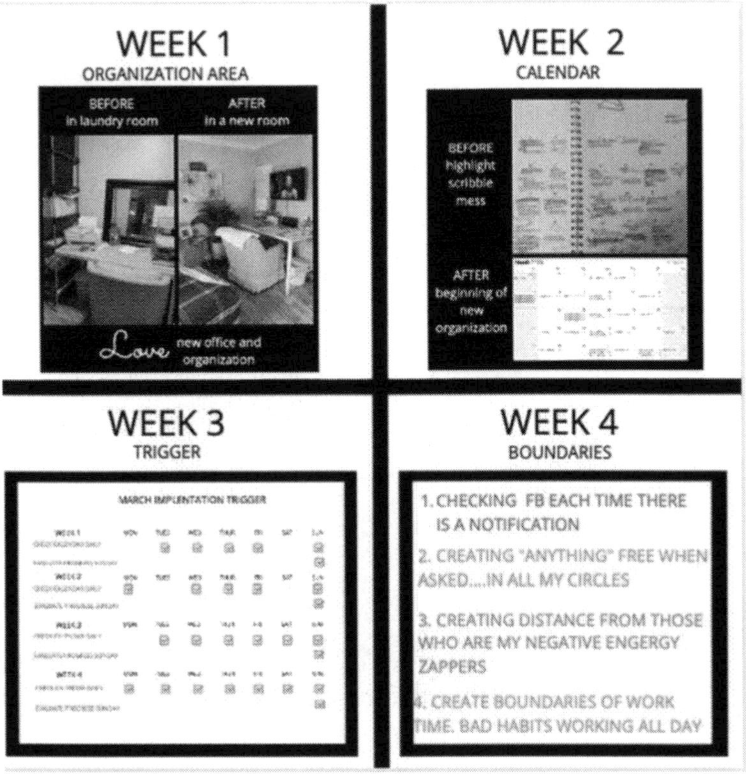
WEEK 1
ORGANIZATION AREA
BEFORE
in laundry room
AFTER
in a new room
Love
new office and
organization
WEEK 2
CALENDAR
BEFORE
highlight
scribble
mess
AFTER
beginning of
new
organization
WEEK 3
TRIGGER
MARCH IMPLENTATION TRIGGER
WEEK 4
BOUNDARIES
1. CHECKING FB EACH TIME THERE IS A NOTIFICATION
2. CREATING "ANYTHING" FREE WHEN ASKED....IN ALL MY CIRCLES
3. CREATING DISTANCE FROM THOSE WHO ARE MY NEGATIVE ENGERGY ZAPPERS
4. CREATE BOUNDARIES OF WORK TIME. BAD HABITS WORKING ALL DAY

Kristin Kotzebue

"The Intentional Implementer™ Mastery Program was the kick in the pants I needed to get organized and create a system to help me be more productive!

"Creating a calendar and decluttering my schedule and space were things I had on my list for a while but never took the time to do it.

"With this program, I gained the knowledge, the support, and the deadlines to actually take action, and I feel such a weight off my shoulders! Thank you!!"

Laila Ruzika

"Love, love, love that the Intentional Implementer™ Mastery Program was included in the Foot Traffic Formula, and it's totally worth paying for it on its own!

"It's really the basics that are so important before jumping into all of the amazing marketing systems.

"I felt somewhat organized before taking this course, but this really helped me take my skills to the next level, and of course, it's helping other people on my team as well.

"You can't afford not to know these skills!"

Megan Dague

"The Intentional Implementer™ Mastery Program trainings have been so helpful and eye-opening! Stacy's approach to organization and habits is so easy to follow and implement yet extremely effective both in my life as a business owner and a mom.

"The Intentional Implementer™ Mastery Program training on creating a more organized space was a game changer! I never knew how much my disorganized chaos was causing me stress and holding me back. Stacy's systems and organization strategies blew me away, and I know now that I've implemented many of her techniques and created a space I enjoy being in, it will be *so* much easier to work and get things done.

"I normally consider myself to be relatively tech-savvy and good with my time, but Stacy's calendar training made a *huge* difference in how I structure my day. I would have never thought to build things into my calendar or even take the time to input things into my calendar at all! Now I get alerts, have time scheduled and set aside for the important things, and know what's truly important in my day.

"Stacy's training specifically on habits was particularly ironic for me. We do a chore and behavior chart for our son to encourage his good habits, yet I never thought to implement something like this to establish good habits for myself. Now when my son fills out his chart for the day, I fill mine out at the same time. My habits are still a work in progress, but I know seeing my colorful calendar inspires me to do better.

"Boundaries have always been hard for me as a people-pleaser. Stacy's words have stuck with me and made me realize that my own behavior was often the cause or multiplier of any boundary issues. Once I knew this to be the case, it was so much easier for me to correct my actions and be willing to stand up for what will truly move me forward in my business and life.

"Stacy's Intentional Implementer™ Mastery Program trainings are gold. The organization, strategy, and tips are so insightful and actionable. I can't wait to see how my business and life will change and grow from this course!"

Claire Dennis

"Listening or going through a training is always exciting to learn new things. Going through an implementation program requires work! But having the Intentional Implementer™ Mastery Program makes it feel like you know the answers, you know what to expect, and it's something you have access to do! Implementation is what separates the 'been trained' to 'I'm going to implement that'!"

Grace Kwak

"I love this training. This training is all about getting a strong foundation to move forward. Sometimes we are too busy to follow new strategies to grow our business. However, this training will help everyone's work hours cut down to half but with a better outcome."

Jeorgiá Brown

"Intentional Implementer™ Mastery Program was amazing! I especially loved the trainings related to office organization and calendaring. My office is unrecognizable now and everything has a place. I also now have a way to easily coordinate appointments with clients and partners without all the back and forth. Game changer!"

Sara Turack

"Wow. I only wish we had done these changes sooner. Honestly, having Stacy hold my hand for each major area and then hold me accountable has made such a huge difference. I really think implementing these things was the difference between my family and business surviving through this time and thriving. We are thriving."

This is just a small sampling of the success my clients have had in the Intentional Implementer™ Mastery Program.

For more details and how you can put this to work for you – unlocking the secret to getting it all done – visit: www.implementationcode.co/implementer now!

Case Studies

About the Author

Stacy Tuschl has made a name for herself as an expert in growing small businesses. Put it this way: Stacy started her own business at the age of 18 in her parents' backyard and turned that company into a multi-million-dollar business she still runs today. (The Academy of Performing Arts has two locations in her home state of Wisconsin.) In addition to being a Small Business Growth Coach, Stacy is a best-selling author and founder of the Foot Traffic Formula – helping small businesses around the world get more customers in the door, more profit in their pocket, and more happiness in their homes.

When local area businesses started asking Stacy how she grew her company so rapidly, it sparked the inspiration needed to launch "The Foot Traffic Podcast." Her podcast now has over 1 million downloads and is frequently on the top 30 of all marketing podcasts on iTunes. She's interviewed leading experts like Suze Orman, Dave Hollis, Jasmine Star, and Amy Porterfield.

Stacy was named the 2019 Wisconsin Small Business Person of the Year by the United States Small Business Administration. She was featured in *Inc. Magazine* as one of the top 10 podcasts for moms looking to grow a thriving business and has also been featured in the *Huffington Post* and popular podcasts like "Online Marketing Made Easy with Amy Porterfield," "Eventual Millionaire," and "Social Media Marketing."

Stacy lives in Milwaukee, Wisconsin with her husband, Kent, and daughters, Tanner and Teagan.

Made in the USA
San Bernardino, CA
15 August 2020

77073177R00075